WINGS TO BUSINESS IDEAS

JOURNEY TOWARDS ENTREPRENEURSHIP

CA PANKAJ TANEJA

Contents

Acknowledgements

Acknowledgement and Gratitude

First and foremost, my sincere bow to Lord Ganesha for this beginning and to Lord Hanuman for the courage to sharpen my skills.

It was my grandparents, who introduced me to the beautiful world of stories and books and imaginations. My grandfather had shown me this world on his shoulders and taught skills at an early stage of life.

My parents, Reshma Taneja and Harish Kumar Taneja, who have helped me in every phase of life and motivated me to pursue my passion at every stage.

My sister and Jijaji, who have always been there, showering love and for being pillars of support in my life.

My team members, Jay Shankar, Amit, Pankaj, Gauhar, and others, who were always available at standby mode to keep the momentum of work life balance.

My friends, Amit, Hitesh, Ankit, Ashish, Paras, Rakesh, and others, who fought with the world to be on my side so that I could take the important decisions of my life.

Kedar Panda, who motivated me to complete my book with his constant guidance.

Janki Thakkar, the magician who waved wand and gave life to this book by completing it in every sense. Without her inputs, I could not have done what I did.

Thanks to Sneha for cover designing and formatting.

My sincere thanks to my clients, who have chosen me to transform their business and connecting with me not only professionally but also personally.

My sincere thanks to my friends in government departments for their valuable feedbacks and helping me with the research.

Thanks to many people who have directly or indirectly contributed towards the creation of this book. Last but not at all the least, everyone who has appreciated and read what I wrote, and who will read whatever I write. Your validation is the reason I am here.

Introduction

Sachin Mehra was working in the world's most reputed mobile manufacturing company and earning a handsome salary. He was having a lavish house with all possible amenities, and even had a full-time house help named Paras, a 28-year-old villager, besides other staff.

At the age of 35, Sachin was among the essential key persons in the finance field and was awarded twice as 'The Best Employee of the Month' by the company's Chief Executive Officer (CEO). In addition, he was eligible for a bonus equal to the salary every quarter. In short, he had reached a pedestal in his career, which was like a dream for most of his colleagues. Besides having a successful career, his personal life was also great. He was in love with a beautiful girl, and they had decided to get married within six months.

Unfortunately, life took an unexpected U-turn for him. Suddenly, he got a severe stomach-ache. Little did he know that a mere stomach ache would turn into something disastrous. In the initial days, he thought he was having gastric problems due to his unhealthy eating habits. However, when it continued, he had to undergo a few tests. His world was shaken by the results. The doctors said that he had a kidney failure, which was working only at twenty-five percent of its capacity. The only solution was to replace it soon. However, to do that, he needed a lot of funds, a donor, as well as stability in health conditions. Unfortunately, none of them seemed to be possible in the foreseeable future.

His colleagues and management were equally staggered by this news, as he was the mainstay of the company. After the diagnosis of his health condition, everyone in the company started supporting him with day-to-day activities after office hours. He was overwhelmed by the compassion shown by his colleagues, as he had to go for dialysis every third day and was not able to contribute even half of what he used to do before. Over the days, his work allotment in the office started declining. It was now assigned to other colleagues. Feeling guilty, Sachin attended the office as much as he could. But since it was difficult for him to cope up with even the basic routine, he needed a constant assistance. This is where his house help, Paras, stepped into the picture. Sachin had to bring Paras even to the office for taking care of him, providing food, helping him do menial jobs; basically, with everything.

It was during this time that Paras started observing the office atmosphere. His dream of becoming an entrepreneur, which had been buried for a long time now, awakened. While tending to Sachin's needs, Paras would share his thoughts with Sachin. He would lament, saying how he wished his circumstances would have been different! Then, he would have studied better, would have the appropriate knowledge and skill set to start something of his own. Sachin was intrigued and inquired what did he have in mind. Paras revealed that his dream was to launch of a variant of rice, making it fat free, so that people would be able to consume it without having to worry about the nutritional aspect. This continued for a long time. Whenever Sachin would be at ease, Paras would share about his ambition while Sachin would marvel at his thought process, realising that even though he had not attained formal education, his inquisitiveness and urge of gaining knowledge was impressive. In turn, Sachin encouraged Paras and tried to tend to all his queries. A special bond had formed between Paras and Sachin by now, as Paras was serving him wholeheartedly.

Meanwhile, Sachin's career was going downhill. In a span of merely three months, he was left with no work in the office. Then one day, the HR department called him and requested him to resign with three months' bonus salary. They reasoned that they have no work that can be allocated to him due to his ill health. So, it would be better if he left voluntarily, or else after a specific period, they will have to fire him. This was a huge blow for Sachin. He was left with no option as his medical bills were already too high, and the insurance company's limits were also exhausted. Unwittingly, he accepted that he could not work at full capacity.

After knowing about his job status, his fiancée broke their engagement. This was the last straw for Sachin, who now felt disheartened. He had no choice but to settle for what life offered him. At that time, he realised his mistake of not following his dreams and not making his vision come true.

What Lesson Did Sachin Learn?

Sachin learned that if someone has the capacity to do something prominent in life, and still, if he compromises for a smaller goal, then at some or the other point, he is bound to regret his decision. But why was Sachin unable to execute his ideas, and instead invested himself so deeply in other's business that he got so many awards and applause? The reason was that he did not have a plan or steps to implement his idea, and let it go as a dream for others to fulfil. Sachin spent his life fulfilling someone else's idea and forgot about his own ambitions and aspirations. He knew that though an individual can initiate a business, he cannot run it on his own. For this, a team needs to be established, a process has to be followed. And the vision and the process has to be followed by each one in the company, only then you can sustain in the market and make your mark. Sachin didn't have the guts to take up this Entrepreneurial Journey and instead chose the safer path of doing a job under someone, fulfilling someone else's dreams while letting go of his own. And till the time his health was fine, he never regretted his decision; in fact, considering it wise, as financially, he was doing well.

But Sachin had now understood the ways of the world. He knew that the day you are incapacitated to fulfil the duties, you will be chucked out. Years of dedication and loyalty would be forgotten in minutes. By now, he knew that people only liked to be associated with success.

He was no longer in a position to continue with his luxurious life, as he was left with no job. Also, the medical bills were eating up on his savings. All his staff had been long disposed of, with only Paras left with him, as he refused to leave his side in such a condition. This moved Sachin, making him realise that Paras was a true gem. Now that he was left with nothing to do, he thought that the least he could do to repay Paras for all his care was to help him live his dream. He decided to guide Paras such that he could at least execute his idea and make it a reality. Sachin had given a deep thought to the idea Paras had discussed with him again and again about wanting to prepare fat-free rice by removing all oil contents from rice. Being a financial consultant, Sachin was not in a position to offer him monetary assistance but he had the knowledge and the right links to support Paras in setting up a business to attain his aspirations. And he was determined to give it a go.

CHAPTER I

Idea to Outcome

"Just because you made a good plan, doesn't mean that's what's gonna happen." - Taylor Shift

• • •

Sachin called Paras into his room and detailed him on how he would help him in the execution of the idea of fat-free rice. However, Paras didn't pay heed, saying that he had no money, knowledge, education, or any other attributes, which would help him to sustain in the business and scale it. He questioned himself about how it would be possible for him to perform under such circumstances. But Sachin explained to him that to start a business, the major factor that is needed, is courage. Moreover, the moment you have an idea, your business journey begins on that day, although the idea has value only once it is executed. Various factors need to be taken care of while you are on a business journey, but they all are secondary. Thereafter, Sachin shared different methodologies, terms, and stories to help him execute his ideas.

Journey to Business

He explained that the journey to business would be the only way you will achieve your long-term perspective in life - financial freedom and growing your legacy.

Once you start your entrepreneurial journey, you need to form a team, a brand, a product, amongst other things, which help you gain financial security. The one factor you need to remember is that salary always has a limitation. Moreover, the next generation is always ready to do your job more efficiently at a lower price. This ultimately tends to keep you constantly at a high risk. So, to achieve financial security and fulfil the dreams, one should attempt at least once to tread on the journey of business. However, it is important to note that this cannot be achieved by oneself; it requires a diligent team and teamwork, because any business of a noteworthy size cannot be built single-handedly. It not only helps you in attaining absolute security and getting collaboration, but it would also help in achieving your dreams, which you have dreamed of with open eyes.

When you start the journey of doing the business, you should meet a consultant who can help you create an entity that will give a name to your dreams. Always think about starting small. Let's understand how to go about it. If you want to start a factory, then it is better to start with trading. Or if you're going to take a dealership, then it is imperative to have the product knowledge and appropriate training, which will help you in marketing and sales of the products. This will surely give a brief idea of how your product responds to the market. Besides, you will also make a network, comprising different vendors for your purchase and sales vis-a-vis. You will also attain technical knowledge, which is crucial for your growth in this field. In-depth technical knowledge will give you an edge over others, hence helping you to earn extra profits. For example, if a person has knowledge about investments, he will make optimum use of funds, such that he will not only earn profits but also interest income from his funds. This helps you to get significant benefits.

Sachin suggested that we would start a rice shop as it will give Paras insight to reach the final product of the idea. In either case, his customers and suppliers would be the same. Whether the idea is executed or not, it would serve as an introduction to customers, suppliers, and, most importantly, market trends. So, the very first phase of execution of his dreams would be learning business scenarios. Though Paras was not convinced but with Sachin's constant motivation and support, he agreed to open a rice shop at a scale that suited him. Many questions were brewing in Paras' mind. Nonetheless, one thing was evident that if he didn't give this journey even a try, he would surely die inside, and his dreams would be dead.

Sachin's inspirational talks had made him look around with curiosity. Some of the questions that cropped up in his mind were - What if Maruti had not started their journey? Would the world have been able to drive an affordable car today? No, never. Similarly, there were many more inspirational journeys of entrepreneurs, who began their journey which seemed unachievable to others. But you never know if the idea can be a problem solver for the people of the society at large. If the small manufacturers of flour mills, rice mills, pulse mills, etc., would not have gone through their journey, then people may not have been able to eat food. This was the deciding factor. He had to go through the journey not only for himself but the society in general.

No 'Six o'clock' in Business

Sachin explained that although an employee is happy doing nine to six jobs, enjoying and relaxing in his leisure time, there is no such privilege for those who want to do business. You should be prepared to work 24*7, because you are not working only for yourself but also for your team. Your money, mentor, consultant, and employees are working for you, and so you are shouldering the responsibility of many. Business needs constant attention because you have to face numerous problems while you are on the journey.

Think about a business person whose truck with valuable goods is running on the road at midnight to reach a destination, and the sole responsibility is that of the driver. At that time, what will be the mindset of the entrepreneur? He will be constantly worried whether all goods will reach their delivery point safely or not. To make this happen, the entrepreneur will need to give adequate attention to reduce the risk and maintain continuity in business. There are bound to be many such occasions. So, heading a business is a full-time job.

While being an employee, you never bothered about what happened in the office after 6 PM or before 9 AM. But now, when you are on the business journey, you have to think about all aspects of business, and even plan what your team will do from nine to six. Your little celebrations will be when you accomplish small achievements in business. You will keep your eyes open twenty-four hours through internal controls; the rest will be controlled by money itself. Also, if your team is efficient, they will do the work you cannot complete. However, you need to understand that there is an obvious difference between the responsibilities of an employee and the employer. If you are not active besides nine to six, then your business may suffer. Whether there are any mistakes made by the machine or any team member or there is a fault in controls, then such loss will be borne only by your business, and you will not be able to hold anyone else responsible.

Plan before You Jump

If you think that your business is too accessible and will give you money without taking anything in return, then you are mistaken. It is a myth that this world runs only on the concept that the input you provide is the output you get. Similarly, for profit, business needs time and attention in a full-time mode. So, before planning a business, you need immense planning for your margin to be viable. No business works on a long-term goal unless and until it is a problem solver and will benefit the masses. As a business set-up can take time, you must gear up with the resources you will require in that period. This planning will be successful only when you have created financial security for yourself and your family and are ready for a minimum start-up period.

As we are going to start the business on a small scale, it is a calculated risk, since we will never be at a higher risk. What if the plans do not work? You will also have to work on your crisis management, deciding up to when you can handle the pressure of earning low and giving what you have to the business.

Sachin guided Paras that although you will have to put in immense effort, this is the only route for achieving your dreams and fulfil the ultimate aim of your life. Although Paras had not planned well due to his lack of knowledge and means, he had nothing much to lose. Yet, he ensured that in case of failure of his business plan, he would have enough to feed his family at least for a year and spare some contingency fund as per Sachin's guidance. It was a tough decision to make, but he decided to give it a go instead of repenting later for not giving it even a try. Besides, he was having a mentor like Sachin, who was his guiding angel and would teach the art of startup to him.

Art of Start-up

Learning the art of a start-up is essential because it is only based on decision-making. The difference between you and those not going with their dreams is only the power of decision-making. Start-up involves intense decision-making skills that need to be learned, as they will be the guiding factors through the implementation. First and foremost, you should have the ability to plan how to start on a small scale, breaking your idea into small parts. Secondly, the most important thing to learn is to create an identity that will help give a name to your dreams, and lastly, you should know how to execute them. So, in a nutshell, you must give birth to your business, then name it, nurture it with the right ideas, and grow it.

Now the question is, how will you learn about your business? Well, it can only be done through market analysis, either by working at a low scale or getting training in products with some institution. If you do not know your business, you may not earn maximum profitability, and you will also waste a lot of time and money while learning from your own mistakes.

The concepts were new to Paras. So, Sachin thought it best to explain them through relatable examples. Hence, he narrated the following case study:

Pankhuri wanted to start a business in the advertising industry. Circumstances didn't give her a scope to give her dreams a chance. Due to this, she did not get time to work on her dreams. Still, she was pretty sure that she had to work towards achieving her goal. When the urge to do something overpowered her, she formed a company in the name of her parents while continuing with her job. She started marketing her advertising company through her networks and social media platforms. However, she was not able to achieve any advertising contracts for the same. To advertise more at a low cost, she purchased a vehicle, installed a screen over it, and directed the driver to run on roads and stay in public places during peak hours. To her joy, within a week, she got an order for advertising on the screen she was using for herself. Her idea clicked, and she received quite a few assignments, so much so that she had to hire a marketing executive who met the leads and did the formalities before running advertisements on vehicles. After a few months, she reached a comfortable position. There were some backup plans available to her and also some revenues in her start-up. Assured by the progress, she quit her job and expanded her company. She planned her art of start-up and worked towards the growth of her company.

Similarly, everyone has a start-up plan which, if one has the potential and inclination to achieve, works for them.

Why Do Uneducated Excel at Business

We have often seen that uneducated persons are more into business and even successful for the simple reason that insufficient knowledge gives them immense power to take risks. If you don't know, the problems that will come due to lack of knowledge ultimately become the power that will help to enhance the business. Although it is not recommended to start without adequate knowledge, the idea is to learn and execute slowly, as this will lead to lower risk and scale experiences. At the same time, uneducated people never hesitate to learn, because they believe they have an empty glass of knowledge that needs to be filled. So, they must remember that there should never be hesitation in asking. The brain must be trained so that you should never feel guilty about asking anything from anyone. Likewise, we have seen women bargaining in the market. Some even go to the extent of quoting just Rs 500 for goods worth Rs 5000. In such a scenario, if you don't learn the basic tactics, your business will be at high risk. Ultimately, a businessperson should always remember that calculated risk is always better than high risk. Risk is not the only factor in business. Other factors also need to be taken care of.

After hearing about such a concept from Sachin, Paras was amused thinking how his lack of knowledge was a boon. He now recognised the hidden power of ignorance and laughed at himself that being ignorant could also be a strength; he had never imagined this. However, now that he knew better, he decided to start making definite plans to correct everything step by step and gaining knowledge through different modes relevant to him.

Give Meaning to Your Life

We have always known that the happiness behind giving something to someone is indescribable. Imagine providing a solution to a problem or a product to the society. It will give you immense pleasure, ultimately giving meaning to your life. Every birth in this universe is unique, so to find out your purpose in life, start the business. Meaning to your life is only attained when you serve society at large, which is only possible through business. Salaries always have certain restrictions, and the compensation may not fulfil your dreams. To live life to the fullest, you need a lot of money, and that can be earned only with the help of 'Journey to Business'. It is always a matter of pride when you are known by your brand name or product name, which gives you the feeling of owning something brought into this world by you. The happiness you feel is similar to the emotions when you have your first child.

How can you give meaning to your life? It is only when society in general accepts your business as a brand. If you observe, everyone in the house has a preference for a particular brand of spices, flour, pulses, and other groceries we consume. Needless to say, every brand gives life to the owner. For example, we have been using MDH masala for a long time now. Sometimes, I wonder how proud the owner would be when he sees his product in any kitchen. There is no other appreciation which can compare to the satisfaction one feels to see the brand he has created himself being praised for its quality. If you don't live your dreams, you will repent when someone else implements it, lamenting that this idea was mine before a while. I could have been there; I could have done better. There will be only sorrow and guilt in such a case, which is not suitable for your growth in life.

An Idea Should Have a Vision

Dream should have a vision, because when you have an idea with the concept clear in your head, you know where you have to reach, and your mind will work accordingly. Vision is most important as that is the reason a team who works for you comes to you. When you have a clear picture, the consultant or mentors can also guide you appropriately. The benefits of getting the idea's vision are many, but the first and most important factor is that you know where you have to reach. Your mind works accordingly and makes inventory as per the requirement, which will also guide the future steps. When you get into the vision, you know what you have to learn, what you have to arrange, what you have to pick and procure, and what you have to borrow, amongst other things, which will ultimately help you achieve your dreams. When you have the vision, your team member gets a clear direction in what manner and how they have to approach a problem, so that your work can be allotted to someone and they will be capable of decision-making. Ideas can be converted into visions by breaking ideas into a timeline of small steps. For example, when you have decided to start a manufacturing unit, then you can do trading for two-three years. After that, you can plan for a small unit and get a hold on the nitty gritty for another few years. Once you feel that you have a complete command over all the aspects of your business, then you can consider going for a full-fledged manufacturing unit. When you break your idea into definite steps according to the timeline, your team members will also be motivated accordingly.

To learn all skills, Paras and Sachin went to the wholesale market to understand about the vendors, market prices, different qualities, seasonal price variance, availability, transportation, methodology, costing, profit margins, etc., so as to specially build some networks for the product. Then, Sachin explained not to worry and start the small trading firm of specific rice variant only with whatever money he had. Paras agreed to the suggestion and took an affordable shop on rent on his budget.

The next day, Paras went to the market in excitement, prepared to purchase rice with different qualities. However, he had to come back empty-handed because the wholesale market had denied him sales for carrying out business as he needed an entity.

Summary:

- Ideas must be executed, so that later, you don't have regrets in your life. For that, find your vision from the core of your heart and start execution.
- If the uneducated can start a business, why can't you think the same?
- Risk is in the mind. Make a calculative risk and execute it because, at every step of life, there is a risk; whether you travel, sleep, eat, etc., so the least that you should do is, take the risk of fulfilling the dream of your heart.
- Owning a business and being known as the owner of a product you created will always make you proud and successful.
- The people known for their products are invariably called to more prominent stages to help society by making them a leader of the community, which will always hold a special place in their heart; the satisfaction is unmatched.

Activities:

- List your idea and look at the exact nature of the business nearby.
- Make a list of resources that are required to start the business.

- Break down your vision into its smallest part that can be quickly kicked off.
- Ascertain a backup plan for your family till your idea starts generating funds.
- Complete your market survey from purchases to sales, resources to the final product, etc.

CHAPTER II

Entity Creation

"The journey of a thousand miles begins with a single step."
– Lao Tzu

• • •

Paras was clueless about his problem and asked Sachin regarding what a business entity was all about. Sachin explained that a business entity is an organisation founded by one or more natural persons to facilitate specific business activities or allow its owners to engage in a trade. And to understand it better, Sachin explained various factors.

Types of Entities

There are different types of entities. The structure of an entity must be understood before starting it. Also, it's important to note that every entity type has its own merits and demerits. And for this, it is crucial to understand the kind of entity that will suit you. For example, if you are going to start your business individually, then you can choose proprietorship, or if you are going to pursue your journey with a partner, then you can have a partnership firm or limited liability partnership. If you are going to have different types of partners or stakeholders, then you can have a company. You need not be worried that the type of entity cannot be changed for a lifetime. With the scale of business, you can change your entity type from time to time. But it is always recommended to start with proprietorship, as it is created very fast and at a very low cost. On the other hand, partnership takes more time as compared to proprietorship. And also, cost is a bit higher. While forming a company, not only the price but also the compliances increase. This involves cost and documentation, which are tough to handle and understand at the time of start of business. In short, the type of entity depends on the level of delegation of your work. Still, with the nature of your business, it is always suggested to consult a consultant to safeguard yourself from future worries. What if the proper type of entity is not selected? Then, it can cost a lot after a while, and disputes may arise at a more significant level. For example, if you start a business with a partner and go for a proprietorship firm based on trust and other factors, it can result into a dispute with the partner at a later stage. Your entity or legal structure decides about tax rates, liability, paperwork, hierarchy, registration, fundraising, etc.

On understanding different types of entities, Paras asked Sachin about the documents he would require to start his business. Sachin then explained to him about handy documents and certifications.

Handy Documents and Certifications Become the Identity

While forming an entity, we must also inform the government departments at different levels and get the other certifications and licences that apply to your business. Some of the licences and certifications are common, while some differentiate from the nature of the business to abide by the law of the land. So, it is essential to keep your documents handy, which will later become an identity of your business. The type of licence that will be required commonly is a pan card which the Income Tax Department issues and has no relevance to whether your income is more or less than the taxable limit. In cases other than Sole Proprietorship, you must apply a separate PAN for your legal entity.

Secondly, you need Udyam Registration or MSME certification, which will be an identifier of your business. Thirdly, when you have crossed the specified turnover limit depending on your business, you will be required to have GST registration, which will also work as an identifier of a business. At present, GST Registration criteria is based on turnover. Any service provider that delivers services worth more than Rs 20 lakhs in a calendar year is needed to register for GST. This maximum is Rs 10 lakhs in special category states. Any firm involved in the exclusive supply of products with an annual turnover of more than Rs 40 lakhs is needed to register for GST in case of interstate commerce. Regardless of their aggregate turnover, an organisation must register for GST if the supply of goods is done from one state to another. Interstate service companies must register for GST only if their yearly sales exceed Rs 20 lakhs. (This maximum is Rs 10 lakhs in special category states). Moreover, anyone who sells products or services through an e-commerce platform must also register for GST in India, regardless of the turnover. As a result, vendors on Flipkart, Amazon, and other e-commerce platforms must obtain registration before they can begin selling.

Fourthly, depending on the nature of business, you will require a labour licence, factory licence, pollution licence, water test report, soil test report, land conversion, industry licence, boiler licence, and many more, depending on the nature and class of business. How can we apply for such licences in the present era? All licences are mostly online, but in some instances, a visit by an officer is required to verify compliance as per the law. For example, if you have applied for a food licence for a factory, then an officer visits for verification of regulations followed to keep the food safe as per the act. Consultants also help in compliance with the law before the visiting officer so that the act of procurement of licence can be done quickly. There are different consultants for different assignments. Some may be experts in getting a food licence, and some may be able to help better in getting an industrial licence. So, while choosing a consultant for a specific licence, some background checks may be required. If government regulations are not followed, then penal actions can be ordered by the respective department, such as lockdown of business or financial penalties or lockups. Again, the case may be different as per the noncompliance done as per the acts and laws.

Sachin then gave the following example so that Paras would be able to understand it better:

Gaurav had set up a hotel. Now the restaurant and was running full-fledged. He was paying taxes on time, whether it was income tax or GST. Though he had checked about the adherence to the compliances and was satisfied, he had blundered. When he received the notice to present the Pollution Certificate and its compliances, he was shocked as he was unaware of that. He was of the opinion that only large manufacturing units required such things. On observation, he found that his hotel was contradicting with the law framed by Pollution Department. To his utter dismay, he had to shut down his business for three months and make the required modifications to get the licence. He understood that civil construction and management were insufficient to start the business. He also needed permissions from the different departments to start such a business, for example, food licence, pollution licence, trade licence, fire safety licence, labour licence, etc., depending on his criteria and capacity. After procuring such licences, he was able to start his business.

Start on a Small Scale

Business should be started on a small scale, the reason being that at the start of the business, you have insufficient knowledge of the law, market, and technology. When you choose to start small, you learn with the span of time with experiences and by meeting new people in the market. When you start with a small unit, all your costs of creating the entity, compliances cost, number of licences, and other certifications are low. For example, someone is opening a trading shop. In that case, he may not require a factory licence, pollution or boiler licence, etc. So, during the period, while dealing in the product, the entrepreneur gets an opportunity to know the product at a deeper level with the demand of the product based on the nature of the location, etc. He also gets a fair idea of the supplies of raw material and other related products. Thus, before going for a large scale unit, you will be able to know the cost-effective measures of the product at different levels. There is always one question in mind about how to start. The short and simple answer is, the idea should be divided by four. Likewise, if you want to start a business with a capital of Rs 1 crore, then you invest Rs 25 lakhs and think about how to begin. Another alternative is to manage your business with the limited capital as we have discussed earlier.

When you are thinking of starting a manufacturing unit, then you should start with trading. If you want to start trading, then you should go for product training to be able to get optimum output. Similarly, let's take the example of web-based applications. Start with putting your business on similar platforms. Only after getting enough experience from there, over a period, scale it in accordance with the demand of the market. However, if the business is commenced on a large scale, your risk factor will also increase due to the lack of knowledge of product technology and the market. For example, for preparing juice, you may purchase raw materials locally. At the same time, other geographical locations may have the same raw material at a much lower price. This will affect your cost of sale and result in loss.

Paras started from a small scale as advised by Sachin. He used to procure rice from the wholesale market and stock it in the shop. He then delivered the products to different customers, going on cycle, giving them door-to-door service, and expanding his network. After a span of time, even his brother joined him in business, who helped him deliver the products door-to-door.

When to Get Registered

It is also essential to know when and why to register, because prior registration is a costly affair. For example, you may have yet to be in the ambit of GST applicability. Still, if you apply for GST, then unwantedly, you have to pay GST on the sale of the product or services and bear the compliance cost of it. In case of services, GST is not applicable up to Rs 20 lakhs. Still, mistakenly, if you have procured a GST number, then you have to pay a GST from Rs 1, which will affect your profitability. The licences that are needed to be procured and the criteria for which you have to get it should be remembered. Likewise, GST and other licences are based on the turnover besides several other criteria.

For example, if you don't have a boiler, then why do you need to have a boiler licence? If your business is service related, then why will you have an industry licence? If the number of employees in your unit is less than the specified criteria as per ESI and PF, then you will also not pick up such licences. So, it is important to have knowledge about when to register yourself for a specific licence. All this can be done by making a timeline and criteria of having registration, which you need to monitor on a time-to-time basis. When you touch that criteria, you should pick the relevant licence. What if you don't monitor the same? In that case, the business continuity may get affected because when it comes under the head of the government, then the officer may lock the premises or penalise the company for not complying with the respective laws. In order to avail the most benefit out of it, we have to update ourselves with the various government rules and regulations. Also, it is always recommended to take the advice of a consultant regularly to assess the prospective applicability of the laws.

Sachin advised Paras to keep a track on sales value. Only after crossing such a mark, Paras had to get his company registered. Due to such planning, Paras was able to save compliance cost of the same. Besides this, Sachin also explained to him about:

1. Meaning of MSME
2. Government schemes

Sachin guided Paras not to focus too much on the general laws and acts and only update himself about whatever was relevant to his company, as that would have a great impact.

Meaning of MSME

At present, the government has classified Micro, Small, and Medium Enterprises (MSME) on the basis of turnover and investment. In case if the turnover is less than Rs 5 crores, then you will be classified as a micro enterprise. If your turnover is less than Rs 50 crores, then you will be classified as a small enterprise, and if you turn over is less than Rs 250 crores, then you will be classified as a medium enterprise. Above that, you will be classified as a large enterprise. Moreover, as far as the investment is concerned, if your investment is less than Rs 1 crore, then you will be classified as a micro enterprise; if your investment is less than Rs 10 crore, you will be classified as a small enterprise, and if the investment is above Rs 50 crore, then you will be classified as a medium enterprise. Above that, you will be classified as a large enterprise.

The benefits gained by enterprises under MSME also depend on whether the enterprise falls under the micro, small, or medium category. Depending on the scale of business, when you determine the criteria, you will be able to get the maximum benefit of the government specified subsidy schemes. However, if you do not classify yourself, you will not be able to access the schemes of the government, and your margin will be wiped off. For example, if your competitor is availing the benefit of such a scheme but you are not, then the cost of the product will vary, which will directly affect your profit margins. Different ministries have different schemes, depending on the criteria. To cite a few, the Ministry of the Micro, Small, and Medium Enterprises includes schemes like credit guarantee scheme, ISO certification reimbursement, bill discounting schemes, etc. On the other hand, the Ministry of Labour and Employment has Apprenticeship Training, Skill Development Initiative, etc. The most commonly used scheme is the Ministry of Finance Scheme, i.e., Pradhan Mantri Mudra Yojana and Prime Minister's Employment Generation Programme of Ministry of MSME.

Sachin gave yet another example to Paras, which was as follows:

Puja was always worried about plastic scraps, littering the environment and being a matter of grave concern to the landfill issues. At the back of her mind, she constantly used to think of different ways to overcome this issue. Her intention was to recycle such plastic scraps, doing her bit for the social cause. For the same, she planned to set up a Plastic Granules Plant where she would collect thrown away plastic, convert it into plastic granules, and sell it to the industry. But due to lack of funds, she was unable to do that. Then after researching on various means to implement her idea, she took help of the bank and applied for PMEGP Loan. This enabled her to set up her plant. Later, she was also able to get a subsidy of 25% of the project cost, which helped her in reducing the loan burden and managing the project efficiently. Gradually, she got success as compared to the other rival enterprises, due to MSME benefit schemes that she availed.

Government Schemes You Must be Aware Of

You can avail maximum benefit of government schemes only when you know the schemes minutely. And for this reason, the government has also appointed consultants to help you. They will also help you to get different licences from different authorities through a common portal. The office government schemes also define different types of ratios and different investments. Besides, they also help in the set-up of small scale industries. The government schemes have defined ideal ratios and schemes, on the basis of which, different schemes can be availed.

For example, they have specific vendors for different machineries. So, if an entrepreneur purchases from such vendors, he is not liable to only the vendors but also to the government authorities through the scheme of government incentives. He can also procure government related work. For this, the government has made several portals. Mostly, government benefits and schemes are divided into three criteria.

First is the central government which forms different schemes. Subsidies and benefits are provided by central government authorities.

Secondly, the scheme formed by the state government authority depends on the demand and supply as per the state and such subsidies provided by the state government.

Thirdly, such schemes are formed by the local authorities under the state regulations by the municipal, which are provided at lower levels to the vendors. You need to understand all these aspects according to the project you are starting.

Government schemes, mostly Central Government and state government schemes, can be applied in online mode.

Some can be applied directly, while some can be applied through the consultant. This helps in preparing the TEV report. They are the mediator for the project while lower level schemes can be applied directly from the office. Schemes are of different nature, varying in its terms. They may be related to a capital subsidy, interest subsidy, or some may contain electricity subsidy. It is important to know the government subject subsidies because it directly affects your cost of the product. For example, if the government is giving electricity subsidy, then cost of electricity will be reduced to your cost of sales, which will directly result in the profit.

Sachin then gave the following example to shed more light on the concept while explaining it to Paras:

Gaurav wanted to open a rice mill. For this, he did a lot of research in government schemes in context of establishing a rice mill with project cost of Rs 20 Crores. He applied for a capital subsidy scheme in Central Government from where he had availed the capital subsidy of Rs 5 Crores. He also applied for state government schemes from where he was able to avail the interest subsidy for bank loan and electricity subsidy for three years, which are revenue in nature. Due to both the subsidies, Gaurav's business turned out to be profitable right from the first day. Later in the year, with the help of MSME Certification, he was able to lower his interest rate. This always gave him a lot more profit as compared to his competitors.

Basic Laws Should be Known

It is of utmost importance for a businessman to be aware of the basic laws. If any consultant or team mate you hire with the responsibility to update you, does not provide data or not take care of any revised rules, or cut off data, your business will ultimately suffer. The reasons and excuses may be numerous, but nothing will justify the loss your enterprise will have to bear in such circumstance. Therefore, basic knowledge of law is most important for the entrepreneur. Most importantly, you must know the impact of income tax, as based on the slab applicable to you, you can avail benefit. You need to determine under which category income will be taxed, which deduction will be beneficial for you, and also what rebates are available for the business under various sections.

Secondly, you must have an in-depth knowledge about the tax rate applicable to your product. For example, if you have charged GST with the wrong rate, then the difference rate amount with penalty and interest will be paid by you. Similarly, you should also know the different licences you require from time to time. Although you may not require to learn at a deeper level, basics should be known by you because ultimately the profit and loss will be borne by your business.

How can you gain knowledge about the basic laws? Well, you can know only by discussion with consultants because there is a difference in the nature of business of every product. So, it cannot be common for all. However, it is always advisable to have written consulting so that it can be a legal property at a later stage. Alternately, you can also learn the basic laws with the market itself by following the trend preferred by other businessmen at the same level. If you don't learn the basic laws, then you may not be able to do proper decision making for your business. Without knowing the impact at different levels, you cannot identify the price of the product. This is because the cost of the product cannot be computed, the layout of the factory cannot be decided, and the compliances cannot be met, which can affect your business directly or indirectly, sooner or later.

After understanding different concepts, Paras decided that the best approach is to start with proprietorship. With Sachin's help, he obtained MSME certifications and Shop and Establishment licence. Through this, he was able to open his bank account with the trade name 'Paras Rice'. He was able to start the business from scratch with only a few documents. He had to understand the nitty gritty of business, as he was new to it. He also understood that till the turnover remained under the prescribed limit, he would not require any GST Registration. His business flourished over time, owing to his dedication and customer service. However, he again got stuck when a hotel industry denied purchasing rice from him due to lack of licences. Then, in order to understand the same, he discussed it with Sachin.

Summary:

- Once your plan is finalised, then at least form an entity or give a name to your idea you dreamed about.
- There is no need to start with a large unit. It is always advisable to start by taking small steps and make it large over the time. Taj-Mahal was not built in a day; so, don't dream of building an empire overnight.
- Always make a time line when to get registered in each and every department, as early or late registration can cost heavily.
- Have a brief idea about which licences and taxes are applicable to your business and product to safeguard from penalties due to lack of information.

- Government promotes entrepreneurs to conduct business through different schemes. Ascertain the best schemes suitable to yourself and apply for the same. Leave the rest. And remember not to get too dependent on such grants or schemes.

Activities:

- Decide a name of your entity.
- Consider the type of entity which suits your enterprise and which is low in maintenance.
- Meet a consultant.
- Form an entity.
- Acquire licences that are required.
- Start a small trading business when you establish the firm and concentrate on building network.

CHAPTER III

Taxes and Licences

"Taxation is the price which civilised communities pay for the opportunity of remaining civilised." - Albert Bushnell Hart

• • •

Paras had obtained the required licences such as PAN, Udhyog, Aadhar card, to name a few. But he was still not clear about how to transmit returns to the department and which licences need to be procured. To get clarity with regards to this, he was having a discussion with Sachin, who explained that obtaining tax licences is not enough. He also needed to obtain the licence applicable to him and understand how to maintain records and stressed on the importance of due dates. However, Sachin thought it best if he explained about tax applicability first, and then about licences to be procured.

Tax Applicability and its Impact

It is important to know tax applicability as it is directly related to the product costing. Let's take the example of selling rice. When the packaging is less than 25 kg, then it will be taxed at the rate of 5%. But when the quantity is more than 25 kg, then the tax rate will be nil. Here, we can see that there is a direct difference of 5% to the final price. This can affect the decision making of the product and marginal benefits to the entity.

In order to explain the situation to Paras, Sachin gave the following example:

Krishna was based in a small village, where people didn't have access to everything, as it was an underdeveloped village. Krishna saw an opportunity and started trading business. Basically, he purchased goods from the city and sold them into his village. He was mostly dealing with food grains. Then once, when he was bringing a vehicle full of food grains from the city, his vehicle was caught by GST officers. On verification, they found that though his goods were taxable, but he hadn't paid the taxes. As a result, he had to face penalties and prosecution. Ultimately, the business had to suffer. To get out of it, he had to spend a lot of money as well as time. Thus, to have knowledge up to a certain level about taxes is important.

Knowledge about tax applicability helps in determining the cost of the product, supply of the product, transportation of the product, and other factors. If in any case, without being aware of the tax applicability, the maximum retail price is ascertained, then it will lead to losses.

Now, let's consider the direct taxes, that is income tax. If someone is forming a company, then it will be taxed at the rate of 30%, while if anyone is conducting business on a proprietorship basis, then he will get the benefit of the slab rates as per the Income Tax Act. Therefore, such taxes are beneficial for the cash accruals as well. For example, if a private limited has earned a profit of Rs 1000, and he has to pay Rs 300 as income tax, then he will be left with cash of Rs 700 only. While an enterprise having proprietorship has to pay zero income tax for the same, and will be left with cash of Rs 1000. This makes it clear that under proprietorship, an enterprise gets a cash profit of Rs 300, which will affect the liquidity of the business.

Tax applicability must be known prior to commencing the business and prior to selling the product, because if a wrong tax is charged, it will affect the business directly. The best mode of knowing the tax applicability is the market and the other source is the consultants. It is always advisable to have written legal consultations so that how your tax structure has been identified/calculated, can be known at a later stage. If tax applicability is not known, then sudden tax may affect the continuity of the business. As we know, some taxes are direct and some are indirect. If indirect tax is not collected by the source of consumption, then the entity has to pay the default amount, which can be huge. For example, a product is having a tax rate of 5%, and mistakenly, it has not been charged on the invoice. Now let's say the total sale of the company was Rs 1 crore, then at the time of assessment, the entity would have to pay Rs 5 lacs with interest and penalty from own funds.

Different Types of Taxes

Taxation is at different levels for the simple reason that the money is used at different levels. Some taxes are charged directly because it is possible to calculate and pay them, while some are charged indirectly because it is not possible to calculate and pay them. Tax is collected to make the product available to you. For example, if the roadways don't exist, then how will the goods reach you? Therefore, such tax is used to develop the infrastructure, so that the product can be made available to the consumers with an ease.

Officially, the taxes have been divided into two parts - direct taxes and indirect taxes. As the name suggests, direct taxes are directly collected by the entity, whereas indirect taxes are collected by the consumers. Direct tax mainly comprises the income tax, and indirect tax includes GST and other local laws. In some cases, taxes are levied prior to GST. Different states have different laws, which can be confusing and tough to understand. It becomes strenuous to abide by the different laws. But with the introduction of GST, all states are on the same platform. The taxation has become a little easy, and it is not too much of an effort to comply with the same.

GST is levied on the basis of the product and the nature of business. The tax rates vary with the products and nature of business. So, taxation totally depends on your business structures and products which are dealt with. If taxation is not followed, it will result in direct loss to the entity and will also be leviable to the interest and the penalty. Moreover, the business would be at high risk due to non-compliance with the law.

Licences beyond Taxation

Paras was of the view that as long as he paid the taxes, he shouldn't be facing hindrances. However, since the hotel industry had refused to accept his goods, he knew he needed clarity on this. For this, he realised he needed to gain knowledge about licences and understand the importance of the same.

Licencing and certification beyond taxations are important because they make sure that the business done is safe for the society at large. These licences take care that the consumers using the products should be ethically procured. It also ensures that business ethics are followed such that it is safe for the societies. Licences beyond taxation depend on the nature of the product and business. For example, in the case of food licence, it ensures that food given to the consumer is safe for consuming. It verifies whether proper hygiene and proper raw materials/ ingredients have been used by the business entity or not. Similarly, industrial licence checks whether proper work ethics have been maintained in the premises or not. For example, toilets for the employees should be clean and maintained, child labour should not be allowed, women's safety is taken care of, besides similar other things. Similarly, pollution licence is obtained to ensure that no harmful gases or chemicals are released by the industries, as they can harm nearby locality, flora and fauna, water harvesting, etc. Another example is the boiler licence, which ensures that there are no chances of boiler blast, as it can affect the life of labourers working inside. There are a number of labour laws which ascertain the safety of labourers in the workplace.

These licences are obtained from the respective licencing authorities. These licences are mainly obtained with the physical verification of the designated officer, whose role is to ensure that the compliances of the laws are done by the business entities. They also have the right to inspect the business premises from time to time to ensure that rules and regulations have been followed for a period of time. And this must be followed as it ensures the safety of the persons inside the work premises. If these licences are not obtained, then it will be tough to justify the safety measures taken by the business entity. Moreover, it will be non-compliance of the law, which can affect the business continuity. No business can exist or grow without the safety of human beings.

To support his explanation, Sachin gave the following example to Paras:

Rohan is a businessman, who had established a manufacturing unit on a low scale, related to plastic materials. But he was always worried that if in case of any mishappening in the unit, he will be in a huge trouble. Then one day, an employee injured his hand while working on the manufacturing belt. The employee's injury increased Rohan's worries tenfold. Unfortunately, he had to face penalties from various departments, including financial as well as procedural penalties. To avoid future trouble, he started following the best industry practices and also followed the law and acts which were mandatory to be maintained for safety and security of the employees. While obtaining such licences and changes done in accordance with the law, it made him more confident for safety of their business partners. As a result, he was able to do the business at peace and more confidently, trusting the process.

Never Miss Due Dates

Paras thought that all compliances need to be done at the year end only. When he mentioned that to Sachin, the latter thought it was high time he explained the importance of various due dates, so as to save him from different penalties. Sachin also made it clear that if Paras didn't adapt to the new technology and was thinking about tending to all this personally, then most of his time would vanish in doing such things. The best way was to take care of this is doing online, as it hardly takes any time. Sachin also explained the importance of copies of the documents. He stressed about keeping a track on the documents that have been submitted to remember what information has been submitted to the department.

Never missing due dates reflects on the punctuality of a business. It creates a better image in front of the government authorities. There are lower chances of survey or inspection by the departments, because punctuality gives a great message to the officer about maintenance of records and abiding by the laws and acts. To make sure that you never miss a due date, you should know the due date applicable to you for all laws and acts which are applicable to your business concern. Secondly, you can make a team mate or consultant responsible to abide by the due dates. And thirdly, the promoter himself will have to take care and follow up such that those due dates never get missed, because ultimately, the business will have to face the losses. The best way to never miss a due date is by preparing a reminder chart timeline and knowing which return has to be filed in the month. A clear message should be conveyed to your team member that no due date should be missed. If in case the due date has been missed, the first thing you have to face is a fine, which can further result in penalty as well as interest. In any case, the business has to bear the same. In case the due dates are missed, then certain expenses are also not allowed under income tax, which may result in paying higher income tax. In short, in case any return is not filed on time, then the department charges interest, penalty, and late fees, the three swords, which can affect the business.

Online Licencing and Filing

Online licencing and filing are to be done because these are quick in nature. After filing the same, you have the proper acknowledgement. Also, it is now the responsibility of the government to reply within a definite period of time. For online licencing and filing, documents required for the same should be arranged and data needs to be prepared, which must be filed. This data can be prepared by understanding the return formats and the type of information required by the same. After collecting required documents and data, proper procedure needs to be understood and followed. Likewise, in some cases, even though after filing through online mode, department needs to be informed physically or by email. So, it is important to read the procedure minutely. You can do online licencing by yourself. But if you do not have complete information, or do not have the time to do an in-depth study, then you should opt for a consultant. He can help you in obtaining your licences and filing for the same at various intervals. If online licencing and filing is not done, then the onus will be on the entity. It will have to justify that the filing has been done in manual mode on the specified due dates. This can only be done by having the receipts from the department, which is again a tough job.

Copy of Returns and Office

Copy of Returns needs to be maintained and will be required at various levels. Wherever it needs to be submitted from time to time, the figures after submission of return will be the final figures, which cannot be changed afterwards. So, the Copy of Return should be kept at the office. It can also be assessed by the inspection authority, and for that reason, calculations of such returns should be kept handy.

Returns and certification to be kept at the office can be segregated in two parts, such as a permanent file and a regular file. The permanent file will contain permanent licences which are not accessible at regular intervals, such as PAN, TAN, MOA, AOA, GST Registration, Factory licence, Labour licence, Trade licence, to name a few. Secondly, a temporary file or a regular file can be maintained, which can contain monthly returns, quarterly returns, and yearly returns. This will make it easily accessible, as it is required at regular intervals by the team members and inspecting authorities. Such returns and certification should be kept in both modes, hard as well as soft copy, because laws and acts do not contain any provisions to maintain such records in the online mode. And in case it is maintained, then at the time of inspection by the department, they will not allow the time to generate data from the system, because the laws contain the word registers and do not have the word system break downs.

How Much to Learn about Taxes

After hearing about so many rules and regulations from Sachin, Paras was starting to feel demotivated. He exclaimed that being uneducated, it was like appearing for a board examination without having any idea what the laws and acts were all about. This made Sachin laugh heartily. Sachin smiled and patted on his back, pacifying him as he clarified saying that you need not learn all of it. Only gain knowledge about what is relevant to you. The rest time will teach you. Paras felt relieved to hear this and was now keen to understand the concept from Sachin, who explained it in a very simple way.

An entrepreneur should limit himself from learning laws and taxes. As we know, there are monthly returns, quarterly returns, and yearly returns. Now, if an entrepreneur will get engaged in such returns, then when will he do the business? Taxation is a part of business, but without business, taxation is of no use. It is important to understand what is applicable, particularly to your business. As an entrepreneur, you do not need to have the complete knowledge, because in general, laws and acts have a large base as they cover a number of businesses. So the knowledge of only what is relevant to your business is required.

Some basic taxes that can be understood include income tax slabs applicable to them, GST rates applicable to their products and licences, which are applicable to them. Rest all should be outsourced, so that an entrepreneur can concentrate on the business, not on the compliances. This is because compliances have a lot of complexities, formalities, data analysing, and technical issues. Learning all this takes time, so it is better to outsource these tasks.

The best way to learn taxes is by observing the market trends that you get to know through the entrepreneur doing a similar business. You can update yourself about what that entrepreneur is implementing. For further clarity, you can confirm the same with the consultant. In case you don't have clarity regarding the tax rates, then you can also consult the government through Advance Ruling. But once the government gives judgement, it is unchallengeable. It is important to understand that if you do not learn the basic taxes and laws, then planning may not be effective, costing cannot be identified, and you will always fear the government authorities.

Paras now had a clear understanding that due to the lack of the Food licence, his progress had slowed down. Then, on the same day, after meeting a consultant, he applied for food licences by complying as per laws. As soon as he procured the required licences, he was able to sell his rice to the hotel industries. However, an entire year passed by the time he was through with all the processes. Now, he was worried about the tax returns he had to file. So, he met a consultant, who explained to him about the Income tax.

Summary:

- It is always important to know the tax applicability to your business and its impact on the business.
- Direct tax impacts the cash flow of business as it is directly paid by the business, while indirect taxes are collected from consumers and deposited to the governments.
- Due dates of every act must be followed to save one from late fees, penalties, and interest. Missing a due date means being hit by these three swords at once.
- Compliance cost is much lower than the three swords, so better to keep track of the same.
- A separate set of returns, licences, and important documents must be kept at a registered office by segregating into permanent file and current file.

Activities:

- Understand the taxes that would be applicable to your business.
- Understand licences and procure those applicable while start-up of the business.
- Discuss with the entrepreneurs doing similar business and know about which licences they have procured. Then look for ways to comply and procure them.

- Keep a copy of important documents with you in your mobile device so that information can be accessed as and when required.

CHAPTER IV

Basics of Income Tax

"The hardest thing in the world to understand is the income tax." –
Albert Einstein

• • •

When Paras approached the consultant, he explained the importance of filing income tax and who had to mandatory file the returns. Although Paras was not in eligible criteria as his income was below the taxable limit, he filled his income tax return because he had big plans. He wanted to obtain the bank loans, so these returns would be helpful in the future. However, he questioned the consultant who guided him, and together, they planned the income tax.

Better Schemes in Income Tax

There are different schemes in income tax which can vary with people, geographical location of people, habits of people, etc. which affect the net in hand cash flow. Government keeps on changing taxation slabs and rebates through budget, notifications, and circulars. So, one needs to understand basics instead of going into the exact percentage, as it will change on a year-on-year basis.

Income tax has segregated tax rates according to the type of entity. For Proprietorship, that is, in case of an individual, it is taxed on the basis of slab rates and deductions, which may include insurances, housing loan, etc., while for other business entities such as Partnership, Private Limited, Limited Liability Partnership, Public Limited Company, there is a fixed rate, that is, tax is charged at a fixed rate on gross total income.

Tax planning is to be done on a year-on-year basis with future projections to have maximum benefits in coming years while using different deductions and rebates and choosing entity type. Accordingly, investments or actions need to be taken and can be carried out. For example, there is a deduction under section 80C of income tax for certain expenses and investments such as investment in PPF. If your gross total income is Rs 8 lakhs and you had made an investment of Rs 1.50 lakhs in PPF, then you will be taxed only at Rs 6.50 lakhs. So, in the year you planned an investment of Rs 1.50 Lakhs. You can plan your taxes well in advance through different tools available online and can also use different tax calculators officially provided on the income tax website. In case you are facing difficulties, then you may take advise of the income tax consultants for the same. In case proper tax planning is not done well in advance, then you may result in paying higher taxes, which will affect cash liquidity and can also affect your business profits after tax.

.

.

.

.

.

Income Tax Due Dates

Paras was flustered, wary of missing some important due date and then paying penalty. So, he would frequently call up his consultant to cross check about the due date, making sure that he had all the facts right before going ahead with income tax filing. Being unconfident, he was visiting his consultant too often to file the return. This was hampering the consultant's work. However, he understood Paras' dilemma and explained the concept to him in detail.

Financial Year lasts from 1 April to 31 March. This is the time period in which a person's yearly income is calculated. To know the assessment year in income tax, it is important to know about the previous year as well. The previous year in income tax is the year before the current year. For example, if you are filing an income tax return for the Financial year 2021-22 (1 April 2021 to 31 March 2022) in period 2022-23 (1 April 2022 to 31 March 2023), then here, the assessment year will be 2022-2023, and previous year will be 2021-22.

Income tax due dates have been provided to time bound different returns, to collect the data required by the government at regular intervals, and further, to verify the taxes paid on the self-assessment basis. In general, income tax due date under non audit case is 31 July of the assessment year, and in case of audit case, the due date is 31 October of the assessment year, while the audit due date is 30 September of the assessment year. However, dates of different entity types may vary and due dates are also changed based on the economic environment of the country through budget, notifications, circulars, press release, etc. At present, income tax returns can be filed hundred percent on online mode. Specific forms are available for separate categories, and you need to understand the forms applicable to you that are required to be filled and submitted on the portal. In case of audit, then at first, audit report needs to be uploaded by the Chartered Accountant. Thereafter, income tax return needs to be filled up. Applicability of audit also varies on a year-on-year basis, so before filing an income tax return, it needs to be understood whether the audit is applicable to your entity or not. In case you don't file your return and audit on the due date, then it may be filed under Belated Return with penalty/late fees, depending on the income category and periodicity of belatedness. In case return has been wrongly filed earlier than the due date, then there is also an option of revised return and audit prior to further extended due dates.

Financial Mirror AIS/TIS with SFT

Certain pieces of information are collected by the government authorities through the specified financial transaction reports and other reports, which are reflected on a separate portal of income tax named as AIS/TIS. The information provided needs to be compared before filing an income tax return to ensure whether all transactions reflected are correct and have been considered while filing. The information base is increasing as per the time-to-time change in government regulations, but in general, information reflected are sales as per GST, purchases as per GST, land sale and purchase records, share and mutual fund transactions, cash deposits and withdrawals from bank, interest income, dividend income, commission income, professional income, etc. This information can be accessed by logging in on the income tax portal. If such information is not considered while filing your income tax returns, then it may result in penalty and interest.

Disallowed Expenses in Business

Certain expenses are disallowed in income tax to derive the profit of business on an actual basis, and tax can be calculated on the same. Some of the expenditures which are disallowed while calculating income from business and profession are mainly those expenditures, which are not in relation to the total income, such as personal expenditures, penalties, etc. In case such expenses are deducted while deriving income as per income tax, then such expenses will be added back to the total income. Thereafter, the tax will be calculated on it. For example, if your income is Rs 1 lakh, and you have made some disallowed expenses of Rs 5,000, then your total income will be Rs 1.05 lakhs. So here, we can also identify the difference in taxation profit and actual profit.

Cash Transactions Are Not Allowed

The consultant noticed that in order to save time, Paras was paying the vendors in cash and doing transactions, which are not allowed as per act. However, it was obvious that having no business experience, Paras was clueless that this was considered to be against the laws. So, the consultant decided to make him understand which transactions are not allowed in business.

The consultant explained that cash transactions are not allowed while calculating income from business or profession. This would help in counteracting money laundering and tax evasion, encouraging transparent business practices, enabling the environment for growth of transparent businesses, and easing of auditing and investigations. Any cash expenditures exceeding Rs 10,000 per day are not allowed. Similarly, cash receipt of Rs 20,000 or more is not allowed for any loans or deposits or any amount in relation to the transfer of any immovable property. Receipt is not allowed to be received in cash, amounting to Rs 2 lakhs or more in aggregate from a single person in a day, or in respect of a single transaction, or in respect of transaction relating to one event or occasion from a person. However, some exceptions are also there. If any such transactions are carried out, then such transactions are separately reported in income tax audit reports as well as returns. If such a transaction has been done mistakenly, it has to be added to profits, and total income will be calculated at the derived value. Also, further penalty and interest can also be levied.

The consultant cited the following example to help Paras understand the aspect better:

Atul was doing trading of fertilisers and seeds near the rural area market. He was quite satisfied with the growth and profits he was earning, but he never took care of the taxation part. He was purchasing and selling goods without bothering about the income tax aspect, assuming that everything can be managed. But the day he received the income tax notice regarding clarifications of transactions carried out by him, and about the cash purchases done, he started having restless nights. He was quite shocked that due to his negligence in following business procedure as per the laws, he had to pay tax, penalty, and interest on whatever purchases were done by him. After the tax assessment was done by the department, income tax was auto debited with interest and penalty amount computed by him from his bank account. As a result, his business had a severe cash flow crisis and suffered greatly. Nonetheless, Atul learned the importance of tax compliance at an enormous cost. After this incident, Atul never took irregularities and non-compliances of tax structure for granted.

"Today, it takes more brains and effort to make out the income-tax form than it does to make the income." - Alfred E. Neuman

TDS and TCS - When to Follow

In some transactions, his vendors deducted tax while remitting to Paras. Unaware about the protocol, Paras had an argument regarding the payment, saying it was the income tax department's prerogative to deduct tax. The vendor then told him that he was working as per the income tax guidelines only. This confused Paras, who visited his consultant to understand the theory. He thought that when his business would grow, he would also deduct tax and work on behalf of the income tax department, although all that he would be doing is, fulfilling his duty by adhering to the compliance. The consultant patiently explained what the vendor had done and the laws pertaining to it.

In certain cases, "Tax Deducted at Source" (TDS) and "Tax Collected at Source" (TCS) is deducted/collected to have control over the transactions and tax collection of government from time-to-time. In a similar pattern, advance tax also needs to be paid. The concept of TDS was introduced with an aim of collecting tax from the source of income at the time of receipt of amount, which is likely to constitute income or application of income. As per this concept, a person (deductor), who is liable to make payment of prescribed nature to any other person (deductee), shall deduct tax at source and remit the same into the account of the government. The deductee from whose income tax has been deducted at the source, would be entitled to get credit of the amount thus deducted on the basis of Form 26AS or TDS Certificate issued by the deductor. These were introduced to collect tax at the source from where an individual's income is generated. Items on which TDS/TCS is applicable are professional fees, salary, purchases, commission, sales, purchases, foreign payment, cash withdrawals from banks, interest payment, purchase of land and building, etc. In case of failure to deduct tax or failure/delay in payment of the tax deducted to the credit of government by the due date, it would make the deductor an assesee by default in respect of such tax and also liable to penalty, which is equal to the amount for which the assessee is a deemed defaulter. If TDS and TCS are not deducted or collected at the time of payment, then such a financial transaction is added back to the income. In addition, interest and late fee can further be levied by the department.

Taxation of Loans and Gifts

After understanding about TDS and TCS, Paras now wondered whether he had to pay taxes on loans received from Sachin and gifts/support received from his relatives, as it was his income and tax is levied on the income. The consultant guided him about the same.

Taxation of gifts is important to differentiate between actual gifts or created gifts. For example, if unrelated party gifts are given to anyone, then it will be income as per income tax. If such transactions have not been bifurcated, then all receipts and payments will be in terms of gift, and no income will be shown for anyone. In case of any sum of money received without consideration exceeds Rs 50,000 during the year in aggregate will be chargeable to tax. But in the following cases, monetary gift received by an individual will not be taxable:

1. Money received from relatives (Relatives have a specific meaning)
2. Money received on the occasion of the marriage of the individual
3. Money received under will/by way of inheritance
4. Money received in contemplation of the death of the payer or donor
5. Money received from a local authority
6. Money received from any fund, foundation, university, other educational institution, hospital or other medical

institution; any trust or institution referred to in section 10(23C).

7. Money received from or by a trust or institution registered under section 12A, 12AA or section 12AB

8. Money received by any fund or trust or institution, any university or other educational institution, or any hospital or other medical institution, etc.

In case of a start-up business, if any gift is received by an individual on occasions of birthday, anniversary, etc, it will be chargeable to tax. Although in case of friends' gifts, the money for supporting your business will be chargeable to tax as a friend is not a relative, as per the Income Tax Act.

In case proper treatment of such transactions is not done while filing return, then such an individual will be leviable for a penalty at the time of assessments.

To explain the above situation better, Sachin provided an example:

Sukhvinder is a doctor, who advises patients on a consultation basis and has gained popularity. Now, he has a dream to establish a hospital. When he puts this suggestion to his friends, they offer to pitch in, wanting to become a part of his growth. So, along with his friends, he plans how to expand his business. The friends want to gift their money to Sukhvinder for opening the hospital. Some neighbours also wish to contribute and gift money for the same. But Sukhvinder's consultant restricts him to take any gifts from his friends and neighbours, as he would have to pay a tax of 30% on whatever money he will receive from them. For example, if he receives Rs 10 lakhs as gift, then he will have to pay approximately Rs 3 lakhs as tax, which can affect his dream of starting a hospital. Now, he is in a tight spot, as he realises that although the gifts will be utilised for a good cause, still, he would have to pay taxes on the same. After having discussions with consultants and his known doctors, Sukhvinder decides to form a trust/NGO, where any donation received for the hospital and utilised for the said purpose, will be exempted from the taxation. The efficient planning, with the help of the consultant, will aid Sukhvinder in achieving his dreams, taking care of proper tax planning.

From the above discussion with the consultant, Paras got a good update about how to deal with the income tax issues. And for the GST, he thought of approaching his supplier, who would be able to guide him better as he would have to deal with the GST quite often.

Summary:

- You need to plan your taxes well in advance so that you can take maximum benefits out of schemes available as per the Income Tax Act.
- You should know when an income tax return is to be filed and what is the criteria for getting your books of account audited.
- Prior to finalising books of accounts or filing an income tax return, it must be checked that all the information available with the income tax department had been accounted for or not.
- Every expense or cash transaction is not allowed in business, so while conducting financial transactions, such as receipt, payment, purchases, or sales, compliances should be kept in mind to safeguard from penal actions.
- At every level of growth, income tax applicability also enlarges. So, it is also important to understand when

TDS and TCS will be applicable to business and which procedures are to be adopted while conducting business.

Activities:

- Plan which income tax schemes suit you.
- Write down income tax due dates in your calendar.
- Make a habit of saying no to cash transactions in business.

CHAPTER V

Role of GST in Business

"The best things in life are free, but sooner or later, the government will find a way to tax them." - Anonymous

• • •

Paras had already understood the tax rates applicable by studying the market. And now that he had crossed the taxable limit, he gained knowledge about GST from his supplier who guided him with the major concepts of GST, which should be kept in mind while carrying out business transactions.

GST - A Bliss

Paras was initially apprehensive about GST, but the consultant explained how beneficial it was, compared to the complex system which was prevalent before.

Earlier, there were laws and acts such as excise, VAT, NCCD, etc which required a lot of follow-ups. But after GST, everything vanished, such that now we have almost 'one nation, one tax', and the filing portal of all over India is also the same. However, some of the acts of states remained unchanged. The documents required for GST registration are PAN, Aadhar, electricity bill of premises, rent agreement, consent letter, and the HSN code of the product or services. Also, after GST registration, a bank account is opened with the trade name as per GST, and these bank details are to be submitted at the portal within specified time limit. GST number is a combination of state number,

PAN, number of registrations, and check codes. GST is based on the place of business. If the place of business is in the same state, then such place can be added in GST already obtained, but if the place of business is in other state, then GST number of such state needs to be obtained. This GST registration process is done online. So it can be applied from anywhere for any place. There is no need to visit any office, unless in certain specified cases. If incorrect documents are submitted at the time of registration, then the department will issue a Show Cause Notice, point out the deficiencies, and will give an opportunity to correct the deficiencies. Only after such correction is done, GST number will be issued.

The supplier then gave the following example to Paras to explain the scenario:

Shyam was carrying out business, but he was completely clueless about the taxes that his consultant was guiding him about. He was following it blindly instead of thinking a bit about of it, while his competitors were working with a complete guidance from the consultants and took efforts to understand the law before they pay the taxes. Due to dependency on consultants, he was not able to decide on the tax structure. Moreover, when he was giving a quote to the company for the new orders, due to lack of knowledge, he did not consider the GST cost in the price. At the end, he was able to procure the orders, but ultimately, the tax burden was charged later on, and he had to bear losses on these orders.

How Input Tax Credit (ITC) Flows in GST

GST is a consumption-based tax. So, the concept of the Input Tax Credit is implemented. To make it simple, we can understand it through an example. Let's say, you have purchased goods of Rs 1000. The tax is levied at the rate of 10%, which amounts to Rs 100. So, the final paid amount would be Rs 1100. The selling price is Rs 1100, and the GST thereon is Rs 110. So, the final amount received will be Rs 1210. The GST Payable amount will be derived as received Rs 110 minus already paid Rs 100. Then, the final GST amount that will be payable will be Rs 10 (Rs 110 – Rs 100 = Rs 10).

Such GST paid at the time of purchase will be added in Input Tax Credit (hereinafter referred to as ITC) Ledger, and GST Payable will be subtracted from such ITC ledger. The balance amount will be paid through cash and bank. ITC ledgers are maintained in a similar way to bank statements. Rs 100 will be credited in your ITC ledger at the time of purchase. When you pay Rs 110, then Rs 100 will be debited. Such a ledger will be zero and the balance of Rs 10 will be paid through cash and bank. You must have seen some disputes in the bank that amount was debited but not credited at the receiving end. In such an instance, you complain to the bank about the resolution. Similarly, if your credit ledger is not reconciled with the government calculated ITC ledger, then the department can issue Show Cause Notice (SCN) for reconciliation. In case of non-satisfactory evidence submission, penalty and interest can be levied.

Uninterrupted and seamless chain of ITC is one of the key features of Goods and Services Tax. ITC is a mechanism to avoid the cascading of taxes. In simple language, cascading of taxes are 'tax on tax'. Under the earlier system of taxation, credit of taxes being levied by the Central Government was not available as set-off for payment of taxes levied by State Governments, and vice versa. One of the most important features of the GST system is that the entire supply chain would be subject to GST to be levied by Central and State Government concurrently. As the tax charged by the Central or the State Governments would be part of the same tax regime, credit of tax paid at every stage would be available as set-off for payment of tax at every subsequent stage.

The supplier then explained the concept further by giving the following example to Paras:

Manish was a service provider in the field of technology. Most of his clients were based out of India. So, in order to provide service to them, he was charging GST from them, which he had to bear from his own pocket. After a span of time, he was claiming refund of the same. He had to invest a working capital which had to be given to the GST Departments besides spending resources for claiming refund of the same. Though he was meticulously maintaining a timeline for all refunds, after discussion with his consultant, he identified that there is also a scheme where he need not charge GST on export services by filing Letter of Undertaking (LUT) to the department. After knowing and implanting this, Manish was able to save a working capital amount, which enabled him to earn marginal benefits out of it. So, it is always fruitful that an entrepreneur should understand taxes applicable to him and be aware of the procedures his competitors are following.

Types Of GST Dealers and Returns

We had earlier seen there can be different types of business owners - small, micro, medium, and large. So, according to his criteria, category, and requirement, a person can choose his GST registration. There are mainly two types of dealers - composition and regular. In the case of composition dealer, there is a simple rate of tax without ITC. For example, it is 1% for traders, irrespective of the GST paid at the time of purchase. Such entity had to pay the GST at the fixed percentage, and the tax cannot be collected by the buyer. Also, the GST paid by the buyer can be used at the time of reselling by the buyer. Quarterly CMP 08 return is to be filed, and annually, GSTR 04 is to be filled. The other type of dealer is the regular dealer. Two returns need to be filled in accordance with the present law - GSTR 1 and GSTR 3B. In the case of GSTR 1, an entity has to file all sale records, and in GSTR 3B, computation of tax payment is done, and balance tax amount is paid. You can choose your dealer type at the time of registration, but there is nothing to worry about if the business grows or decreases. Such dealer type can be changed on a yearly basis.

Rates of GST

There are different rates of GST as per the policies, notifications, and circulars decided by the government. It differs frequently, based on the usages, nature, growth, and various other factors. Mostly, the rates have been clubbed under 5%, 12%, 18%, and 28%, and tax has been divided into three parts - CGST, SGST, and IGST. IGST is charged when sale is done interstate, while CGST and SGST is charged when sale is done intrastate. There is a zero rate tax concept in case of export sale, subject to conditions applied. In the case of goods sold at no profit, there will be no GST as per earlier concept. Earlier, in an example, we understood about the goods purchased at Rs 1000 and Rs 100 tax paid on it. In the same way, for goods sold at Rs 1000, the tax charged will be Rs 100. Then, there will be no tax to be paid through cash ledgers.

Now, the question is, how to identify your rates? The best way to identify the rate of GST is through market acceptable rates, through consultants, and in case of doubt, it can also be confirmed by the government authorities. If in case the wrong rate is charged, then the differential rate can be collected by the business entity.

Disallowed Inputs

As we know, in income tax, certain expenses are disallowed. In a similar fashion, certain inputs are also disallowed. Such restrictions are imposed to avoid the input taken, which has no concern with the business. For example, grocery purchased for the home and GST paid on such purchases cannot be allowed. The products and services of the inputs not allowed are mainly motor vehicles, foods, outdoor catering, beauty treatment, health service, cosmetic, plastic surgery, insurance, repair and maintenance of motor vehicles, membership of club, health centre, fitness centre, rent a cab, life insurance, health insurance, etc. However, there are exceptions which need to be understood separately. GST paid on products and services on which inputs are not allowed are directly added in the expenses or assets, and if such inputs are reflected in the GST returns, such have to be reversed. In case such inputs are taken mistakenly, then it has to be reversed in the next returns, and if utilised, then it has to be reversed with interest. If it gets noticed by the department, then a penalty can also be levied.

Reverse Charge

There are some categories, which are having an unorganised market. In such cases, tax has to be directly paid by the entity itself to the department. This is in case of specified cases on a self-declaration basis such as a transporter. Services which are currently covered under reverse charge are transport services, advocate services, etc. In the case of such services, tax has to be paid on self-declaration basis. For example, if you avail transport services and pay Rs 20,000 to the transporter, then in such a case, GST has to be paid at the rate of 5%. It amounts to Rs 1,000, and this has to be paid directly to the department through cash and bank, through help of return GSTR 3B. In the same return, input of such can be taken. If it is not paid on self-declaration and is paid at a later stage, then at that time, input will also not be allowed. So, it is always better to pay timely.

E-way Bill and E-invoicing

To avoid delay in collecting data from the entities and for smooth checking of goods at the time of movement of goods, Electronic Way Bill (E-way) bill is generated. It contains information related to the shipment of a consignment of goods. The details include the name of consignor, consignee, the point of origin of the consignment, its destination, and route.

E-way bill has two concepts - Part A comprising details of GSTIN of recipient, place of delivery (PIN Code), invoice or *challan* number, date, value of goods, HSN code, transport document number, and reasons for transportation while Part B comprises transporter details

(Vehicle number). Just like an e-way bill, a GST Registered business must generate an e-invoice for Business to Business (B2B) transactions. E-invoice is nothing other than registration of invoice at government portal. However, exceptions are there for issuance of an E-way bill and E-invoicing. Such e-way bill and e-invoicing is done in online mode, and there is no requirement of a visit to office. If the e-way bill and e-invoicing is not done, then the department can issue penalties, interest, and legal actions. Also, there can be an issue of data mismatch at the time of filing returns.

The explanation by the supplier helped Paras to determine the way forward. He obtained the GST number and gained knowledge about his tax rates. With compliance and proper networks, his turnover was increasing on a month-on-month basis. But he was still not satisfied. Even after spending two years in this field, his dream of manufacturing fat free rice was lost somewhere. He wanted to achieve the same. Then what was stopping him from growing? Well, the main reason was while handling day-to-day business scenarios, his main goal was lost. But he was feeling restless, so he decided to find the solution to overcome the situation. And for the same, he joined some management courses tailored for an entrepreneur. Here, he learned the concept of getting control through accounting.

Paras' consultant guided him about the income tax while Sachin had already explained that GST registration has to be done at the right time. However, during the initial stage, he had still not been clear when GST registration was required to be done. Besides, he was also facing issues to sell his rice to canteens, societies, etc. In order to solve the issue, he thought it best to understand the fundamentals of the business right from its foundation. He was happy that he had achieved a milestone now as the entity had crossed the benchmark to obtain GST. As such, he knew that this is just the start. His learning journey would pick up speed from this point. He smirked while talking with his consultant over the call that now, he will have to obtain one more degree, "goods and service tax". The consultant laughed, impressed with his approach and positive mindset by terming the licence as a degree. He could see that Paras had come a long way and was always keen on learning. He also felt good that he was helping an MSME entrepreneur grow and achieve his milestones. Paras, Sachin, and the consultant were thrilled to cross every hurdle and achieve one goal after the other. The enthusiasm and guts with which Paras worked was commendable.

The next day, Paras reached the consultant's office to learn the same.

Summary:

- GST is to be collected from the consumer and deposited to the government. So, the correct rate is to be assessed.
- Type of dealer and their returns matter a lot in new business so as to control the compliances cost.
- Correct rate of GST applicable to your product and services must be known to safeguard from future penalties.
- Never risk taking inputs which are not allowed to be taken as per your business, as it can revert with huge penalties and interest amount.
- At what level information is to be submitted to the department must be known, which is mostly dependent on a turnover based criteria.

Activities:

- Collect some sample invoices and quotations of the same product.
- Compare the tax rates that the entrepreneurs in business of a similar nature are using.
- Meet your consultant. Check the rate of GST according to your product.
- Understand inputs which are eligible to your business and which are not allowed in your business.
- Finalise your product cost, considering the tax cost and compliance cost.

CHAPTER VI

Accounting gives you Control

"Accounting is the language of business." – Warren Buffett

• • •

On visiting the consultant, Paras realised the importance of having a good hold on accounting. Since he had nil knowledge about even the basics, the consultant suggested taking up a night course in accounting. Though this was not a cakewalk as Paras would be conducting business during the day time, still, the zeal in Paras to elevate himself didn't let him hesitate in going the extra mile, and was appreciated by both the consultant and Sachin. The consultant then smiled at Paras and said that there's no age bar for fulfilling your dreams or educating yourself. Take every day as an opportunity to grow. So, take the plunge and give it your best. The consultant's motivating words stayed with Paras and renewed his zest to grow in every respect. Without thinking for long, Paras joined the midnight course for accounting.

While doing the course, Paras gradually got a good hold on accounting. He also learned the importance of accounting and how to implement it through different processes and procedures. After completing the course and gaining a thorough knowledge, he explained the concepts to his employees in order to implement the same.

Accounting - A Bliss

Accounting is not merely for recording the transactions, it is way beyond that. It will be the backbone of the business. If at any stage, it fails, then it can lead to failure in confirmations by the other party. Accounting helps in controlling every business cycle, such as purchases, sales, cash book, bank book, inventory register, account payable, account receivables, etc. Several methodologies can be used. At the basic level, the accounting of financial transaction is done very simply. However, when your business grows a bit, your accounting grows at an inventory level, where every movement of stock is recorded. Thus, it helps you in tracking at inventory levels. Also, when your business grows, different accounting methodologies are used for account receivable, account payable, etc., depending on the requirement of businesses. For MSME, any accounting software with an inventory module is a must, as it has every module in smaller formats and helps you keep track at all times. It can even generate the financial statements of a particular phase. Such software is available under Rs 50,000. Some are even free with the GST number. These accounting software also helps in generating returns required by the income tax, GST, and others. There are also specific software in the market. For example, in the medicine industry, batch number and expiry date are of utmost importance. So, the accounting module also gives control on such database, where the movement of goods is recorded from the batch number. If proper accounting methodology is not used, then it can lead to confusions. What's worse, even penal actions can be taken. For example, in a medicine shop, if goods movement batch number records are not maintained, then penal action can be initiated by the drug inspectors.

Don't Fail in Accounting

Accounting is the most important aspect of business; it records and gives you control as well as a brief view of the financial scenario of the business. It helps in recording every financial transaction of business, such as sales, purchase, receipts, payments, etc. While recording every transaction, it gives you a brief picture of the financials of the business. It further helps in the generation of various reports such as ledgers, confirmation, trial balance, profit and loss, balance sheet, etc. It is also helpful in preparing reports required by the taxation body in the form of returns on a time-to-time basis. Every business needs a check-point, and accounting provides you various forms of check-points to control the business, such as credit limit to buyers. If in the accounting methodology, it is standardised not to give more than x amount of credit limit, then at a phase, the sale of goods will be restricted to allowed credit limit only. Accounting has been modernised with new technologies. Therefore, the work of doing accounting separately has been reduced to a greater extent. For example, a Billing Software helps you to account for the transaction at the point of sale only. Preventing failure in accounting is only possible when transactions will get executed once the accounting is done. In other words, no financial transaction will be allowed before accounting. This means, no sales are allowed without billing, or no goods will be dispatched from the premises without *challan*. When you are in business, it is tough to remember each and every thing. At a point, if accounting is not done properly, it will directly lead to financial losses. For example, if the payment is done to the vendor but not accounted for, then it may result in double payments.

Accounting mainly helps in:

- Keeping records of business transactions
- Facilitates decision making for management
- Communicates results
- Meets legal requirements

Now that Paras had gained knowledge about accounting, he explained the concept to his employees by giving the following example:

Ravindra was successfully dealing into the two-wheeler automobile industry for the past ten years. His focus was always on cash profits he earned while completely ignoring the procedural part. It so happened that the government announced to grant a subsidy on the 100CC bikes, having particular chassis numbers. His competitors claimed a subsidy from the government, but Ravindra was not able to claim the same, as he never accounted type of vehicles sold and also failed to maintain the chassis numbers. His competitors then offered price drop to new customers, taking benefit by giving a share of subsidy to the customers, but Ravindra was not able to do the same. In order to solve this issue, Ravindra had to change his mindset. He realised the importance of following a proper method for accounting. He started accounting by implementing such methodology, and for vehicles sold earlier, he had to request the company to share details from their records. He learnt from his mistake, and thereafter, never failed to follow proper accounting methods. Today, he tries to record even the smallest information.

Ledgers and Confirmations

The accounting professor explained about the importance of maintaining ledgers and confirmations in his lecture.

Ledgers and confirmations are important because they are crucial in keeping updated about the balance confirmation from the vendors, who are the lifeline of the business, because if you don't know what you have to pay and receive from different vendors, then it will be very tough to take decisions. In the present era, different ledgers are automatically prepared by the software, so there is no separate requirement of doing the same. The different types of ledgers maintained in general are Assets, Liabilities, Income, Expenses, and Capital. Also, as per income tax, books of account need to be maintained, which include ledgers, Day Book, Cash Books, Account-Books, amongst other books. Such books of account also help in tax planning as well as in various factors of business. These confirmations also help in solving the disputes between vendors and help as a check-point periodically. These confirmations also help at the time of assessments. In case of loans as third-party confirmations, the ledgers serve as the evidence that these are not only book entries. If ledgers and confirmation are not done regularly, then in the future, a dispute with the vendors may arise. For example, if the vendor has deducted some value due to the quality of goods and if it will be known at a later stage, then it can result into a delay in decision making, such as product improvement, presenting your point to vendors, etc. Also, future disputes can be avoided better if there is clarity at this stage.

The accounting professor while explain the concept, then gave the following example to explain his point better:

Sanjiv was a doctor by profession. He opened a clinic near his birthplace. However, soon, he realised the folly of this. He was very tensed due to the number of calls from acquaintances that he had to attend every day. These calls were mainly from the relatives, neighbours, distant friends, officers, etc. for free advisory on their medical issues or someone known to them. He wanted to have control over the calls, which were disturbing and even non-revenue generating. When the situation aggravated, Sanjiv discussed this with his consultant, who guided him to keep an account of the call records as well. Sanjiv was convinced and started keeping track of minutes of the consulting calls and maintained a policy to raise an invoice after three free consulting calls. Once he started following this practice, in a month, the results started showing. He was able to earn money from consulting over the calls and could even save his time.

Financial Statements

Financial statements are important because it gives you a clear picture about where your business is going. It helps you in analysing where the basic defects of business are such that you get an option for correction in business decisions. It is always recommended that it should be checked regularly. Don't just create it in mind; use pen and paper, and follow the proper system.

Financial statements can consist of Balance sheet, Profit and Loss, Schedules, and Cash flow statements. However, financial statements can be differently derived according to laws and acts. Besides, the statements may have some additional notes, schedules, and disclosures. In the present era, preparation of financial statement is quite easy, because it is system-based and all most all software creates financial statements, following a proper method. However, some provisions need to be done for the period ended closure. For certifications, there are different methods which need to be followed. Therefore, it is best to have your financial statements audited by the chartered accountants. Different laws and acts have different conditions for getting the books of account audited. Financial statements are prepared by the system itself, but you have to confirm each and every aspect of the financial statements so that nothing has been left for recording in the books of accounts. You may need some skills in finalising books of account. Certified accountants are accepted worldwide for this job. When financial statement has been prepared, it needs to be reported at various levels for verifications such as income tax, GST, labour licences office, electricity board, etc. Everyone has a different perspective to see the financial statements and derive different results out of it.

Different Ways of Computing Profit and Loss

Profit and loss are different in nature because the purpose of viewing the statement differs from entity to entity and person to person. Some focus on profit and some on cash profits. Profit and loss can be accrual in nature, i.e., all revenue which has been generated and all expenses which had been accrued or committed to pay, will be recorded whether it has been paid, received, or pending. Profit and Loss statement can also be prepared on the basis of receipts and payment, i.e., only those transactions, for which, revenue which has been received and payments have been done, are considered as cash profit. It can also have another way of cash accrual. A Provisional Profit and loss are ad hoc statement, which are unaudited in nature and have a provision of change, which may vary from 5% to 15%. Such provisiona profit is important for the banks to know the profitability prior to closing entries, if any. Projection Profit statements are for the period which has not been completed or are for futuristic periods. It is a statement which summarises the future profitability scenarios in different situations. Further, different tax statutes define different methodologies of deriving the financial statements to calculate the profit and loss as per the laws and acts defined. Different ways of profit and loss are prepared by knowing the statutes and purpose of preparing the statements. It can only be prepared by knowing the detailed reason for preparing such statements. If different profit and loss are not prepared, then computation of tax liability may differ, ratios may differ, projections may not be accurate, etc., which are not good for financial health of the business.

Difference in Assets and Inventory

Everything that you purchase is not for selling. For example, if you buy a home, it is not for reselling. There are several similar purchases done, which will ensure future benefits. These include assets like machinery and furniture, which are purchased with the intention of not reselling, such assets will be clubbed under furniture. Let's say, you are in an automobile industry and you had purchased a car for business use, then it will be a fixed asset. But if you had purchased it for reselling, it will be clubbed with the inventory. So, you need to understand the difference between inventory and fixed assets in your business. This segregation is important, because assets are depreciated while inventories are not. There are different depreciation methodologies, such as Straight Line Method, Written Down Value, etc. This depreciation is important because the value of any asset which is purchased is bound to reduce at a later stage. If it is not done, then you may have not derived the proper profit, which will guide you through asset generation later.

Books of Accounts

Book of Account is to maintained for various purposes such as government authorities, self use, internal controls, banks, government authorities, decision making, shareholders, etc. Books of account may include purchase book, sales book, cash book, bank book, etc. It may enlarge as per the requirement of the law. It may also contain salary sheet, wages register, and attendance register for labour licences. So books of account criteria are not limited only to financial statements; it expands as per the requirements occasionally. In the present era, these books of account are maintained in the online mode. Almost every standard software provides the mechanism of providing the books of accounts as required by the respective laws. These books of accounts also help in fetching the required data for returns. If these are not maintained, the continuance of business becomes a little tough, and a lot of manpower and cost will be wasted to fetch and prepare data at regular intervals. Smooth functioning and optimum use of resources is possible only with proper accounting.

After completing the accounting course, Paras was able to understand the different aspects of business. The time and effort he had invested in doing this course was paying off as he could now see where he was lacking to run and grow the business besides the product and marketing. He started implementing it in his day-to-day business affairs and was able to maintain the books of accounts on his own. Also, now he had three mentors – Sachin, the consultant, and the accounts professor. However, his business was stuck as he was not having enough funds to purchase stock variants and earn the bulk discounts offered by the vendors. In order to understand that, Paras decided to visit his bank and discuss it with the banker.

Summary:

- Preparing a system for every process is a must, and for that, an efficient methodology is required to record each and every business transaction.
- Although you need to incur expenses for accounting, it helps in saving resources through numerous factors, either by reconciling ledgers, payment of taxes, or scrutiny, etc.
- Proper accounting can only help in deriving actual financial statements. In case of even the slightest mistake in accounting, it can lead to losses at different levels.
- Basics of accounting is of utmost importance in business because it is the only rope which controls the business horses. In its absence, business horses will run out of control and will lead to the places which are not so important.
- The more perfect the accounting, the more ethical will the business be. Besides, more data will be available for proper decision makings at various levels.

Activities:

- Identify the process you are adopting or have adopted in your process.
- List down every step from the scratch.
- Find the best practices.
- Change your processes which suit your business.
- Re check again and again after implementation of the same.

CHAPTER VII

Banking and Borrowed Funding

"Good banking is produced not by good laws, but by good bankers."
-Hartley Withers.

• • •

Paras' banker was the chief manager in the nationalised bank. Paras explained his journey of starting from the small to the bank and asked for help from the banker in achieving his next mile stone. On Paras' request, he guided him about the different aspects of the banking and also explained about the schemes available as per the bank and government policies.

Types of Bank Accounts

There are different types of bank accounts, because the usage of bank accounts differs from person to person. For example, a salaried person will have a very low number of transactions as compared to the business executive. So, different types of accounts are customised by the bank at regular intervals, as per the usage of the customers.

There are mainly four types of accounts:

1) Saving account. Here, the bank provides interest on the bank balance maintained, but the number of transactions allowed per month are limited. No sale and purchase transactions are allowed in this account. It is usually opened in the name of the person.

2) Current account. In this type of account, the bank does not provide interest on the balance maintained by the customers. However, the bank allows more number of transactions in a month. These accounts are mainly opened in the firm's name, on which, the customer is carrying out the business.

3) Cash Credit Account. This is the account, where the bank provides a certain limit to the customer and charges interest on the limit sanctioned. Customers are bound to route their turnover from this account.

4) Overdraft Account. This account imposes certain limits on the customers, but gives flexibility to the customer to route their turnover from other accounts.

There are numerous more types of accounts available. So, prior to opening an account, you should understand the nature of the account you require. If you choose the wrong nature of account, you may have to pay the extra cost for the same as bank charges or bank interest. You may also face difficulties from the income tax. For example, if you rotate your cash turnover from the saving account, then after it crosses Rs 10 lakhs, the bank will inform the income tax through Specified Financial Transaction (SFT) return. At a later stage, income tax can investigate the reason for the same.

Varieties of Loan

There are different varieties of loans, depending on the purpose of usage of the loan. For example, a loan may be required for the asset creations, or for purchase of inventory. Accordingly, loans of different types will be required.

Mainly, there are two types of loan: Term loan, and Limit loan (Cash Credit/Overdraft). Term loan is the loan mainly provided for asset generation, such as plant and machinery purchase, car purchase, house purchase, etc. The repayment of this loan is done on an Equated Monthly Instalment (EMI) basis. The other loan type is the Cash Credit (CC) limit, which is used for working capital. Working Capital is equivalent to Current Assets minus Current Liabilities. It can be computed in the following way:

Account Receivable	XXX
+ Inventory	XXX
+ Cash and Bank	XXX
Total Current Assets (A)	XXX

Bank CC	XXX
+ Sundry Creditors	XXX
Total Current Liabilities (B)	XXX
Working Capital (A-B)	XXX

SAMPLE FORMULA

In most of the cases, 75% of the value of the stock will belong to the bank, and 25% of the value of the stock will be of the borrower. You can apply for these loans directly to the bank or through different portals which work as an intermediary. The documents required differ from the type of the loan and amount of the loan applied for. However, some common documents required are PAN, ADHAR, ITR, GST Returns, and Financial statements. If property is given on mortgage, the documents of such mortgage are required as well. From bank to bank, borrower to borrower, and scheme to scheme, loan documentation may differ. If in case the proper type of loan is not chosen, then the business may get affected. For example, if you had taken loan for inventory and opted for a term loan, then with a span of time, loan will reduce, and simultaneously, your capacity to maintain inventory will also reduce.

When Paras looked a bit confused, the banker explained it to him by citing the following example:

Sameer was dealing with confectionary items in his own building, but he was not happy with the size of his business premises. So, he approached the bank for a loan in order to achieve his goals. Sameer was desperate to receive money for new premises by any means. In order to achieve his target amount from the bank, he agreed for Cash Credit, where the loan amount will be used for working capital. But the purpose of the loan was to build assets. Anyway, Sameer had received funds from the bank as Cash Credit, but he was not able to maintain the desired working capital. So, the bank levied penal charges for change in purpose of loan. Moreover, the income tax did assessment, stating the reasons for stock below the working capital limit. In order to correct this, Sameer had to increase the working capital in the firm by infusing his own funds, which had been reserved for future emergencies. As he didn't know and learn about the type of loan fund and other factors, Sameer had to lose money in way of penalty from various authorities.

Handling Loan and Renewals

It is important to handle loans carefully, because a major portion of net profit is taken by the bank itself. For example, your gross profit is 20%, and you have taken loan on interest at the rate of 12%, then you will be left with 8% of the net profit. Hence, a major portion of your profit ratio is dependent on the bank interest rate. Also, one thing to be kept in mind is that if you get delayed in renewals and submission of documents, the bank may charge penal charges which may affect your profit capacity. So, discipline is a must in business. Documents required for renewals of loans are similar to the documents provided at the time of sanction. The bank also checks the health of the business through financial indicators, mainly known as ratios. If you ask how to handle loans, then it is always suggested to handle loan at a personal level when you are in the criteria of micro and small industry, while when you are at a medium or large level, you can approach through a consultant, because they are experts at bargaining and getting benefit for the owners from different banks. If you are not able to handle loans properly, then you may have to face various penal actions by the banks, which will directly affect the profit of the company.

Importance of Credit Rating, CIBIL

The bank uses the Credit Information Report and other rating systems to ensure how will you do the repayment of the loan taken by you. Taking various accounts into factor, a credit score is generated, which is important for assessing the loan from the bank. This credit score needs to be carefully maintained because it helps to provide the data to the bank, on the basis of which, the bank provides the loan. You can analyse your Credit Information Report yourself or with the help of agencies. It also helps in accessing proper pay load. If your Credit Information Report and ratings are not properly maintained, then the bank can reject your loans and even call back the loan already provided to the borrower.

Ratios and other Indicators

Ratios and other indicators are important because they ensure the health of the business. For example, if the net profit is showing loss, then bankers cannot ensure their future repayment and can deny the loan. So, the bank and other institutions look for certain ratios before providing loans. One indicator is Maximum Permissible Bank Finance (MPBF). It is the method of working capital assessment, which is assessed on the basis of turnover and working capital. Variations to this output vary as per banking schemes and guidelines. Different ratios are derived from Credit Monitoring Arrangement (CMA Data) report, such as gross profit ratio, net profit ratio, current ratio, stock turnover ratio, debt service coverage ratio, debt-equity ratio, etc. Another important calculation may involve 'drawing power'. It ensures the working capital amount that needs to be maintained by the borrower.

Particulars	Amount in Rs
Inventory	5,00,000
Accounts Receivable	5,00,000
Total	10,00,000
Less Accounts Payable	2,50,000
Working Capital	7,50,000
Less Margin say 30%	2,25,000
Drawing Power allowed by bank	5,25,000

EXAMPLE

All these are monitored when you prepare the financial statements at regular intervals. Also, the bank helps to continuously check the financial health and gives you early warning signals. In this case, the bank works as the free consultant of the business. In case ratios are not maintained, then loan can also be reduced by the bank. For example, a borrower is having a CC of Rs 10 lakhs. Accordingly, the borrower needs to maintain Rs 12.50 lakhs of inventory. If he fails to do so and maintains an inventory of, say, Rs 10 lakhs only, then the bank can reduce the limit up to Rs 7.50 lakhs.

Primary and Collateral Security is Required

In case of other than specified government or bank schemes, all loans need to be backed by certain security, which consists of primary security and collateral security. These securities are kept by the bank to ensure repayment of the loan. In case of default, the bank recovers from such securities. Thus, primary and collateral securities are the backbone of the loan. Banks have empanelled advocates, who verify these securities with the help of documents provided by the borrower, which may include property papers, title deeds, land receipts, municipal receipts, maps, etc. After verifying the documents, the advocate submits the report to the bank, whether the property is eligible for being kept in security or not. Verification of securities provided is done occasionally, as per the bank policies and nature of security, to ensure that the legal rights of property have not changed in the period of loan given to the borrower. To further ensure the repayment, bank mortgages such property in favour of the bank.

There can be different types of mortgages, but the bank mainly uses either simple mortgage or equitable mortgage. In a simple mortgage, the agreement is registered between the borrower and the bank, while in case of equitable mortgage, the title deeds of the property are given to the bank. Legal verification is done by the bank, only through the approved bank guidelines with the help of empanelled advocates. In case legality of property is not cleared by the borrower, then the bank can even reject the loan application or may reduce the loan amount.

The banker gave the following example to Paras to explain the context better:

Vijay was having a retail shop of grocery items and he was working at the same pace for quite a long time. However, he was unable to grow himself due to lack of funds; whatever he earned was used as household expenses. The only thing that was growing was the turnover due to price inflations and other factors. Now Vijay wanted to overcome this stagnancy. To solve this, he was in requirement of funds. Though he tried to collect funds from his friends and relatives, he was unable to do so. Then a friend advised him to approach the bank. Though hesitant at first, Vijay knew he had no option. When he visited a public sector bank and explained the situation, he was surprised that the bank was ready to give him loan on security by the government, that was up to Rs 2 crores, but he availed a loan of Rs 20 lakhs. With this loan, he was able to expand his business and earn more. From then onwards, year-on-year, his growth rate doubled. The bank was also supporting him due to his satisfactory performance in the banking transactions. Eventually, he realised that availing the bank loan was the best decision he had taken.

Valuations

A bank does not provide the loans only on the basis of legal documents and financial reports. Valuation of security provided also needs to be done, which identifies the value of loan coverage as per the bank norms. Documents required for valuation of land and building may include Purchase Deeds, Approved Plans, Latest Electricity Bills, Property tax Receipts, Photos, longitude and latitude or boundaries, etc. Later, physical verification may be done by the certified valuer. For this, the valuer may take time of one week per property and submit the report to the bank. This valuation can only be done by the valuer appointed by the bank and as per the policy of the bank. Valuation is mainly dependent on the average of market value and government value. However, valuations completely depend on the bank policies and guidelines. In case value is not properly assessed, then loan value may be declined, which may affect the project.

After discussing with the banker, Paras started arranging for the desired documents for bank finance. But as he was facing problems, he requested his mentor, Sachin, to help him with the funds and in arranging the documents, so that his business could expand such that at least his shop could operate full-fledgedly.

Summary:

- Understanding the nature of the bank accounts you open and the nature of the loan procured is inevitable. After knowing the same, accounts and funds should be utilised accordingly.
- In case of an enquiry of loan from financial institutions, the credit rating declines, which can affect business funding limits. So, prior to enquiry from any institution, the type and amount of loan required must be ensured.
- Securities are important factors in loan. Before you decide to mortgage the property you are living in, you should think over it again and again, because that property will be at risk of your successful business.
- Valuations of securities decide the quantum of loan allowed by the bank. Therefore, only projections and legal formalities are not enough for the loan. Bank security valuations play an important role, because in case a moderate amount of loan is procured from the bank, then the project may get hampered.

Activities:

- Open a Current Account with documents prepared by consultants.
- Identify the purpose of the loan, if required.
- Discuss with your banker about different schemes available with the bank and find the best ones that suits your business scenario.

- Apply for loan and keep the process in continuance, because whether you receive your loan or not, the banker will make sure you maintain the documents perfectly at every stage.
- Utilise the fund smartly.

CHAPTER VIII

Outside Fund or Liabilities

"Debt is like cocaine. It will kill you if it becomes a habit. Equity is like carrots. It will make you healthy if it becomes a habit." —Raghu Venkatesh

• • •

Although Sachin was having a tough time due to his health issues, Paras asked Sachin to invest in his business as he was doing well. Moreover, this would also help him in tending to his medical bills. Sachin had witnessed Paras' growth over the time and had the same opinion. Being an investor would help to keep his mind distracted from his medical tragedy also. As such, in that span of time, his health was stable. So, Sachin decided to invest in Paras' business and give himself a chance again. He saw this as an opportunity to give wings to his passion with Paras' dreams. Nonetheless, Sachin wanted to explain to him about the importance of raising funds. He explained the difference between the outside fund or liabilities, which helped Paras to understand the different funding opportunities.

Types of Shares/Funds

Other than bank loans, funding can also be arranged through other sources. For that, there are different types of shares and funding options, depending on the purpose of fund required. The outside funds are the baseline between borrowed fund to owned fund. Different levels of percentages with different names have been assigned.

Borrowed fund ------------------------------- **Owned fund**

0---------100%

The main types of funds, which are primarily used in the simple business scenarios, are equity funding, debt funding, and government funding. Each type of fund has different pros and cons. Equity Funding is the funding through sales of shares or ownership, so the entity will not have a pressure to repay it. On the other hand, Debt Funding is the funding through borrowing a sum of money, which is further repaid with interest at an agreed future date. To decide the proper fund, your business requirement needs to be understood, and accordingly, such fund is gathered. Let's understand from the point of view of a new firm. When a firm has just commenced, it is better to have the borrowed fund, because at the initial stage, the valuations of the firm will be very low. If the decision is not taken at a proper level and time, then entity may lose its ownership with a lower valuation, which may affect the business.

Creditors' Fund

Creditors' fund is the most important in business because they are mostly interest free till a specific time, although they keep you under pressure to refund, which has a high probability of creating business. There are various types of creditors' fund. For example, at the time of having transaction, you may have a deal of higher repayment period with some higher cost of product, or you may become the sole distributor of his product which will help more. Rely on your business model. He can provide a higher credit period as you will also market his product side by side. Moreover, you can have a deal where the supplier gives his goods for a certain period. Here, if the goods are not sold in the stipulated time, then the supplier can take back his products any time. This methodology is used in the market. It also varies with the relations of the entity with the suppliers. A period of credit terms varies, depending completely on the nature of the product, availability of the product, cycle of the product, relationship with the supplier, etc. In general, the market trend of 30-90 days is prevalent. In case of earlier payments, suppliers also provide cash discounts. The most important benefit of this model is that it is interest-free and a little easily available. But here, the catch is, this model can be implemented only when you create a healthy business relationship with the suppliers. If this methodology is not used, then your profit percentage may decline. Let's assume that your competitor is using it and taking the advantage of early payment. This will help him to earn cash discount, which will directly impact your business. The most important factor that needs to be taken care of is that in case there is a default of payment, then you may not have the availability of the product, and in such a scenario, market reputation may decline rapidly.

Sachin then gave the following example to Paras so as to explain the concept properly:

Amit was doing food grain business from the past two years with high turnover. In spite of such a high scale, he was not able to achieve the desires growth while his competitor was earning more profits than him even at a low scale. His problem made him question his business processes. Therefore, he started to find out the drawbacks in his business processes while comparing with others. What astounded him was that his processes were more effective than others, but still, his profit was low. In order to understand the situation and increase his profit, he hired a consultant. After analysing the facts, he deduced that his competitors were taking benefits of cash discount of 5% by making early payment or advance payment to the suppliers, while Amit was investing spare funds in fixed deposits, which was giving a monthly return of 0.5%. Hence, the difference of 4.5% was creating the disparity. After changing the methodology and understanding the creditor's fund or payment terms, he was able to earn marginal profits.

Creditors' Schemes, Discounts Need to be Understood

It is of utmost importance to learn the benefit of creditor terms, because if you don't understand this, you may not earn marginal benefits, which others are taking benefit from. There can be several types of schemes and discounts, such as cash discount, trade discount, quantity discount, quality discount, bulk discount, etc. Its nature can also vary according to product and its availability. But it is also important to understand the capacity of repayment before choosing any scheme or discount. For example, if you had selected a target discount but failed to achieve, still, you had done sales considering the same, then it can lead to losses. It is a beneficial scheme because it will lead to make a difference in the market with different offers. If it is not taken care of, your purchase price can be on the higher side, which will lead to a benefit to the competitors.

Do You Need Shark Tank Partners?

It has now become a trend to add investors and scale the business by utilising the investors' money. But the question is, do you need an investor? This question needs to be self-answered, because ultimately, you can lose the ownership of the child you had given birth to. Things to be kept in mind while adding investors depends on how much you believe in your business model and sacrifice level. You can think about going for such big investors only after you have scaled up your business to a certain level, as otherwise, it is not investable for them. Mostly, investors look for target market, competition, revenue model, financial projections, funding requirement, future potential, etc. The different funding methodologies a business can use are Bootstrapping (Self-funding), Crowd Funding, Angel Investment, Venture Capital, Business Incubators and Accelerators, Bank Loans, Government Schemes, etc.

The upside of exposure to Shark Tank is that you get to negotiate with the self-made multi millionaires, who have a huge fan following. These investors, if interested in your products, help you to scale your business. They not only help you to overcome financial obstacles, but also reduce the pressure to pay. In addition, business receives valuable expertise, motivation, inspiration, and morale, confidence in stakeholders, and a connection with small federation. Other than that, investors can be approached through the networks you have, like different agencies who work as consultants, internet-based capitalist, social media platforms, etc. Be sure to be ready with your plan before approaching investors. If you do not approach the investors at the right time, then you may have to face a delay in operation of business. In the meantime, there is always a possibility that your competitor will initiate a business with a similar idea and gain traction by breaking your monopoly, thus expanding his business. The probability that the competitor may grow at a speed which can cause a huge hindrance to your existence in the market, is always there. Hence, approaching the investor at the right time is of utmost importance.

Now let's assume that as an entrepreneur you have approached the shark tank. Whether the shark tank offers investment or not, when your pitch is viewed by millions of viewers, you have pitched your business to thousands of investors, a few who may get in touch with you. Besides, you have marketed your product to the public. So, if your product is good, then you get innumerable customers.

Crowd and Social Funding

Crowd funding technique can also be used. This means raising money from friends and family. You may take small amounts of money from several members or close friends to raise a more significant overall sum. They can provide interest-free funds, or you can have friendly investor agreements in the form of rewards. This methodology is used during the early phase of starting a business. The major benefits of this are it is a less formal approach and full control of business besides others. Nonetheless, it also has disadvantages. You have more responsibility for positive returns, more stress in case of non-repayment on time, strain in personal relationships and quality of life, etc.

One major problem which is bound to happen is that in case of disagreement, friends and family try to interfere in business decisions. It is always sensible to have written repayment terms and contracts for any investment. Also, be ready to deal with all problems sensibly and professionally. Such a funding can be approached by presenting your plans to friends and family and ask for their advice as well as support to business by lending money. If these fundings are available and not used, then you may have to pay higher interest cost initially, which can be saved and instead used in the set-up of your business.

When to Pay Dividends

No equity is free, because every investment done by any investor is to gain profit out of it. So, it is very important to decide when to issue dividends, as it affects business health. This is because profits retained lead to take the business to another level. Dividend policy must be aligned with the business goals, which can maximise its value to the investors. When a business gets into profit, then the dividend, i.e., the share of profit must be distributed among the shareholders as a return on their investment. There can be different dividend policies. Some examples are Fixed Percentage Dividend policy, Variable Percentage policy, Irregular Dividend policy, No Dividend policy, etc. While deciding dividend policy, future plans of the business must be kept in mind. If proper dividend is not issued, then shareholders can lose interest in the investments.

Sachin gave a very apt example to support his explanation that he gave to Paras:

A Private Limited company owned by Ritesh wanted to start a manufacturing company in his village. His main objective was to open a flour mill in his area, as it will not only generate employment but also help in the growth of the village. But when Ritesh approached the bank for the loan, his loan was rejected initially due to lack of proper security which was required to give to the bank. Ritesh was stuck midway as the land development plan was done, the project was prepared, machinery advances were made, but now he was having no fund to put his dreams into reality. He tried to make partners in the business but none of them agreed for the same as the unit was located in a village and none could see the scope in such units. Later, Ritesh decided to generate fund by issuing equities to the local villagers. So, he gave them an offer to purchase the equity of the upcoming unit. Within a span of seven days, all his equity was sold out. Surprisingly, all were purchased by the villagers themselves. After arranging such a fund, Ritesh was able to set up the manufacturing unit and successfully run it. After the set-up, several banks came up with different offers, but for now, Ritesh's requirement had been met. In case of further expansion, Ritesh decided that he would opt for borrowed funds.

Office Tools and Search Engines Will Guide, but You Have to Work

Office tools and Search Engines can guide you about different approaches but are not action oriented; actual work can only be done with actual decision makings.

Initiating a business requires funding, so it is important to map finances before starting, such as saving salary, spending less, crisis management, family responsibilities, etc. There should always be a gap between business fund and personal fund, as the family is the backbone of you as well as the business. In case business can be managed on a part-time basis, then it can be planned in that manner only, or in case you want to have a business which can be managed by the employees or any team member in the initial phase, then the job can be continued. By working overtime, business can be reviewed. Different funding methodologies should always be in mind because any business is bound to face a lot of uncertainties. In case planning is not done properly and actions are not taken accordingly, then personal life along with business can face huge losses. But it is also to be kept in mind that if you focus more on office tools and look out for business, then your business will remain only a dream. The chances of success are very meagre, because these mediums can motivate you but cannot replace you.

Paras took funds from Sachin and also from the market to expand his business. The response in the market was too good because he was having deep product knowledge. Eventually, he thought to expand further, but he was not having any idea on how to go about it. In the meantime, he was able to sell his product by repacking it under his brand name, which also gained attention in the nearby areas.

Summary:

- Funds are the important factor of the business. To scale up the business, you have to always decide how much

ownership is at risk and compare it with the cost of borrowing.
- Other than borrowings or sale of equities, there are other options to generate funds, such as creditors' fund, crowd or social funding, etc. So, if these options can be availed rather than sale of equity or bearing cost of borrowing, it will be more profitable for the business.
- Dividend should be issued judiciously. This is because the business generates assets. The dividend can be preponed or postponed with the time schedule of asset generation or making an impact on business scenarios.

Activities:

- Make a list of crowd or social funding, which can be utilised.
- Discuss your projects with different sharks, who can not only reject or accept you but can also provide their expert opinions free of cost.
- Ask about schemes and cash discounts available with the suppliers, in case of early payments.

CHAPTER IX

Things to Know before You Grow

"There is no finish line. There are only mile markers."
- Michael Ventura

• • •

By now, Paras had expanded his business and was supplying rice to more customers. When he received order from one of his past employers, he thought it would be respectful to go personally. But he was taken aback as he was treated in the same way when he was a household staff. This misbehaviour pushed Paras to reach such a height that no one would dare to look down upon him. It was time for him to start the journey to achieve his next milestone. He had already attained success in what he was doing and had gained knowledge enough to start with a bigger self-owned brand with his own manufacturing unit. It was time to realise his dream which he had seen, which was to manufacture fat free rice. This time, he had support from Sachin, the consultant, the banker, different vendors, a strong customer-base, some of who even had links with the authorities. He discussed the pros and cons of his expansion plan at this stage. When all gave a positive response, he went one more step ahead by forming a private limited. For this, he wanted to register his company with his brand name and discussed with his consultant to understand the different aspects of forming a company.

Register a Company

When you have been operating on a small scale for a span of time and have learnt the ropes of the business, you wish to grow the business to the next level. Moreover, you need a brand name, and for that, you can go for the registration of the company. When you own a product which is socially acceptable, then the need of the hour is to have a brand name that the society can associate with. In order to establish a trust factor, you can register a company. Unless you need investors' fund or want to dilute your ownership, stay focussed on what you are doing.

While explaining to Paras, the consultant cited the following example to stress on the importance of taking a well-informed decision at the right time:

Manish thought of starting a business as a technology provider. On the first day itself, he decided to form a private limited company. Although his consultant guided him to form a company after setting up, he didn't pay heed. The so-called 'online knowledge' had brainwashed him and he was rigid to form a company, which he did. With the passage of time, he was not earning a lot but due to the formation of the company, his compliance burden was too high to maintain. Eventually, he stopped adhering to compliances. As a result, after a few years, he received several notices from various departments. The compliance burden was so much that he couldn't pay attention to his business. Ultimately, he had to shut down his business and get back into the job. By the time he understood the value of his consultant's advice, it was too late.

To register for a company, you have to procure certain documents. These include basic KYC Documents such as

PAN card, Aadhar card, bank statements of directors as well as shareholders, electricity bill, digital signatures, besides some other declarations. Along with the documents, you need to provide the list of directors, list of shareholders, name suggestions, percentage of shareholding, the main objective of business and conditions, if any. After registration, you will have the Certificate of Incorporation (COI), Memorandum of Association (MOA), Article of Association (AOA), PAN, TAN, ESI, PF, Import Export Code (IEC), GST, etc. Once the required documents are collected, you can visit a consultant, who can help in compliances and get your work done with an ease. In case the company is not registered, then building the trust factor at a global level will be a bit difficult and acquiring equity investors in business will become troublesome, too.

Burden of ROC Compliance

The consultant explained that one should take into account the fact that with the formation of company, compliances increases as there is an addition of stakeholders in the business. In general, ROC compliances also vary according to the size and type of the company. It depends whether the company is private limited or public limited, listed or unlisted, etc. But in general, you have to regularly submit financial statements and other reports to the Registrar of Companies in their specified forms and formats with verification from certification agencies like Company Secretary, Chartered Accountant, etc. Every decision made in the board meeting, which is an essential part for the stakeholders as specified by the law, must be informed to the ROC. This includes notifying important decisions like the change in directors, raising capital, etc. In case the company is formed at a larger scale, a Company Secretary needs to be hired, who can adhere to the ROC compliances and essentials meetings, as specified in the act. In case the ROC Compliance is not followed, the ROC may initiate a late fee, penalty, or even prosecution if required, depending on the severity of the noncompliance.

Although after forming the private limited, the burden of compliance was enhanced but Paras was not concerned as he was having enough savings to manage the same. As such, he had almost outsourced all this burden to his consultant so that he could indulge in setting up his manufacturing unit. He started investing his time and energy in to the project with a vengeance, making him unstoppable. The in-depth knowledge about the licences to procure, loan procedures, return filing system, market trends, procedure to get subsidies, etc., helped in setting up his manufacturing unit without any hurdles.

Public View of Data - Positive or Negative

In case of a company, various stakeholders such as shareholders, directors, and different departments are involved. So, for the benefit of stakeholders, ROC has given option for public view of documents, which may be prove to be beneficial at times while in some cases, it proves to be troublesome. Information generally available for public view is the date of incorporations, last annual general meeting date, last financial statement date, present directors, company address with full details, and loan taken from bank with specified payment of *challan*. Besides, all other information such as financial statements, changes in directors, loan documents, and other details, which are submitted through ROC filing, are also available such that in the minimal time, anyone can access the desired information. This public view of information can be taken from the MCA website. Also, there are different aggregators, who make the desired document available from MCA. The company has no control over the information and cannot keep it hidden. This is an important decision taken by ROC to make it possible for the public to view documents, even though it is a private limited company.

Transfer of Business

In case there is a probability of transfer of business, then the best option in such a case is a company. As we know, a company is owned by the shareholders, so by a change of shareholders, the company is transferred. There is one important aspect that by transfer through company, identity of the company, that is important documents such as PAN, GST and other identities, remain the same. However, it is not the case with the proprietorship concern. Documents required for transfer of the company are basic KYC documents, fund transfer as per the valuations, and a couple of ROC forms with some payment of fees. Its procedure is simple and can be completed within a couple of days. The filing also does not take too much time to fulfil the compliances. In case transfer is not done through the company, it may create legal compliances in the future. For example, in partnership, in case of improper change in partners, there may be dispute of goodwill calculation, which varies a lot.

Asset for Income Generation

After the factory was set up, Paras was eager to share portions of profit with the shareholders. That is when his stakeholders gave the following explanation and asked him to manage the funds wisely.

Once a company is formed, then with the help of further investments, it can be enlarged. Judicial investments in the cost of a project will further help in generation of income, which includes land and building, plant and machinery, technology, etc. Such cost of project should be compared with the means of finances such as the owners fund, borrowed fund, and government subsidy. After the means of finance is decided, vendors can be finalised from whom such assets will be purchased. Thereafter, proper steps should be taken in a planned manner.

Project set-up and licences should be planned well as it will ensure smooth set-up of project. The basic issue that needs to be sorted is time, because there is a high probability that there will be a delay in projects as everything does not work according to plan. There may be a delay due to a number of reasons, such as transport delay, labour shortage, licencing problem, etc. One of the key factors may be technological problem. It is very crucial that the plant and machinery are properly set-up and sync in a way that it provides maximum production. The most worrisome is the fact that for any reason, if the project is delayed, you have to bear the interest cost under any circumstances, which can be a burden at a later stage. It should be always kept in mind that after taking a loan, its utilisation should be done timely and appropriately to control interest burden and unknown pressure of banks. If there is any problem in the project set-up, you can ask the bank for assistance. The bank can help you in obtaining different licences and technical issues, if any, as they have a network with different persons and have funded such projects earlier as well, so their knowledge can be used accordingly. In case the project is not implemented properly, the best way is to inspect it timely and correct it as soon as possible.

Internal Controls

After the project set-up, the next factor is to develop internal controls and work on every business cycle to automate each and every aspect of the business.

When the business is small, many roles are played by the owner; it's like a one-man show. Internal control is not so important as all the functions of the business, like procurement, inventory, sales, paying the bill, receiving the money, etc., are managed by the owner. However, as the company gets bigger, especially on corporate levels, many functions are divided and done by specific departments and personnels and are managed professionally.

Internal controls should be maintained at every level. For example, from entry of raw material to exit of finished goods. Each and everything should be system based on the premises.

The next level of control should be the financial control, such that each and every penny should be spent only after checking and dual authentication, not by quick decisions.

The technological controls should be taken care of at a very proper level as the lives of humans are involved. If precautions are not taken at every step, then the workers' lives would be at stake.

The next level of control should be the movement control. Every movement should have a policy, whether it is a paper or machines. This internal control can be done only through the help of identifying and implementing policies and procedures properly at every level of the business. It can also be better done by knowing best followed principles in the businesses of a similar nature. If proper policies and procedures are not maintained, then it will be tough to control and business may suffer losses due to inappropriate decisions. Policies and procedures are guidelines to lower levels for decision makings.

"Spend time upfront to invest in systems and processes to make long-term growth sustainable."- Jeff Platt

The consultant had explained the importance of the above technicalities quite well. In order to explain it better to Paras, the consultant mentioned the following case study:

Jitendra set up a mid-sized animal feed factory. He allocated different personnel for different tasks but did not lay down the policies and procedures which form the internal controls. After a new personnel joined the finance department, he observed that there was always a shortage of funds for buying raw materials. He assumed that his revenue cycle was lagging due to the late collection of funds. However, his myth busted on the day a farmer came complaining to him that he did not want to pay 1% commission for instant pay for supply of raw material. It was then that he realised that in the absence of any procedures laid by him, the suppliers had to bear the 1% commission, due to which his supply of raw material also declined. From that day itself, he laid down the policies and procedures to build internal control and rechecked it stringently at regular intervals.

The knowledge shared by the different stakeholders gave an insight to Paras, who followed the procedures and was able to set-up his manufacturing unit of rice, working for the society at large.

Summary:

- Getting a larger-than-life status is not as important as growing from small. Because higher status always entails high compliance cost, which is bound to affect business directly or indirectly.
- Forming a company is easy, but its pros and cons must be analysed to identify factors at various levels.
- Every penny spent must be for asset generation because it will benefit the entity from a long-term perspective.
- Growth is not possible without forming a process through internal control systems. So, it should be

embedded in to the business regularly and should be reviewed in between periods.

Activities

- Identify whether your business is based on the brand name of whether it can operate with lower compliance cost.
- Download different financial statements of similar nature of business and study the strategies adopted by them.
- Read the history of the company's growth through financial statements and apply their positive points into your business.
- Read in depth about asset generations.
- Go through internal control benchmarks and apply into your business.

CHAPTER X

Satisfaction and Automation

"Everyone wants to live on top of the mountain, but all the happiness and growth occurs while you're climbing it." –
Andy Rooney, Journalist

• • •

Once the manufacturing unit was successfully set up, the stakeholders, mainly, Paras, Sachin, the consultant, the banker, and some vendors were present in the first AGM of the company. All were congratulating Paras and praising his journey so far. Though Paras was immensely happy, he did not let the success get into his head. His focus was on the step he had to take further and he started planning for the next milestone, which would be accomplished only through his stakeholders. When he shared his plans with those present at the AGM, they were jubilant. The experienced stakeholders guided him about the way forward as under:

Importance of Business Network

Once the project is set up, then you will understand the importance of the procedure you followed for achieving the vision. The power of the business network you created during the earlier stages will help you at every level from procurement to sale. The people from whom you had been purchasing the goods, will now sell your branded goods.

This will benefit your business family, which has grown big by this stage. They will also help in making availability of scarcity problems such as labour, funds, godown, to name a few, and solving your problems in business operations. This network can be maintained by visiting them frequently and taking their feedback seriously by giving proper time to hear them. If you are not able to maintain your business network, you will not be able to achieve further goals/vision on a timely basis.

To support his theory, the consultant gave the following example to Paras:

Hitesh was a dealer of different types of oils and was well known in his area for his retail supplies. Everyone knows about him and his punctuality in business. For the past ten years, he always opens his shop at nine in the morning and shuts it at nine in the night. His staff may be on leave on festivals and holidays, but he never took a leave. This behaviour was also pulling back his growth due to lack of social networking. He never realised the importance of meeting new opportunities, as he bound himself to his work. On asking Hitesh why he spent so much time in the business, he had a standard answer - if he will not take care of the business, then who will? In fact, Hitesh was not knowing anything about the automations, system, and controls because of it. His family was also not happy with his behaviour. Gradually, he realised that something was amiss. In order to enjoy his life after business, he met a consultant. As per the consultant's guidance, Hitesh optimised the process, which let him monitor the business till his satisfaction. After automation, Hitesh was able to enjoy life as well as find new opportunities for his business, which led him to grow to a different level.

Never Trust Anyone with your Trade Secrets

You should always have one thing in mind that under any circumstances, your trade secrets should not be revealed, as these are the only differentiating factors. For example, Coca Cola has till date not shared its trade secrets, which is helping it to be at the top of its game. As an entrepreneur, you need to understand that if you let it out, then your profits will be hampered and your competitors may get more options to make their business profitable. The trade secrets can be related to technology, resources, experiences, or any aspect of your business. You can share trade secrets only by discussion with trusted persons, mostly stakeholders. If the trade secret is not maintained prudently, then the competitors' numbers will soon grow in the market, which may affect the profitability of the business.

Business Culture

There is an utmost need of a proper business culture in the business, because it helps in decision-making. Everyone should be aware of the vision of the company and can strongly adhere to it. If you look into any super successful company's website, one thing is common - their vision is stated on the website. The vision is clear and simple such that every personnel in the company can understand, relate to it, and coalesce, helping the company to achieve that vision. The business culture should motivate and guide the employees towards achieving the vision of the company by adhering to the policies and procedures of the company. Some of the visions and policies and procedures help in forming a business culture. One of the known corporate clients has adapted to this culture in his office, where all the employees get mandatory leaves for family trip during Diwali. They realise the importance of happiness and connect the family with the business, which helps a lot. Business culture can only be implemented if the employer implements it himself; if it is followed by the promoters, then it will be followed by everyone. In case someone is not adhering to the business culture, then there should be a system of penalising, so that the importance of following the rules can be stressed upon. If some decisions are not taken on time, then ultimately, loss will be borne by the business, and it will flow to every team member of the business.

A Close Look at the Business Cycle

It is always important to have a close look at the business cycle, because that is the area where marginal profits lie in the business. Every business should understand their own system and implement the same. What are the types of business cycles?

- Revenue cycle - *The revenue cycle is a method of defining and maintaining the processes used for the completion of an accounting process for recording revenue generated from services or products provided by the company. These include the accounting process of tracking and recording transaction from the beginning, normally which starts from receiving an order from the customer or entering in agreement with the customer, delivering an order to the customer, and end with getting payment from the customer.*

- Payment cycle - It is a series of processes involving the company's purchase and payments department and carrying out all necessary activities from placing an order to suppliers purchasing goods to making final payments to the suppliers.

- Purchase cycle – It is a series of processes involving business need identification, suppliers list creation, supplier selection and contract terms negotiation, purchase order creation, receive the goods and services, reconciliation, and making a payment.

A closer look into the business cycle can be done only by giving time. It should be reviewed periodically. However, it can also be covered in the process of audits. If a close look into the business cycle is not followed, then it may result in losing marginal profits.

One of the stakeholders gave the following example to explain the above theory:

Gyanchandra was having a bakery. He remained so busy in meetings with different vendors, customers, etc., that he was not able to identify the process business was following. At every step, he was confused about the cash flows in the business. In order to resolve this issue, he decided to hire the consultants who could help in writing the process to be followed by the business. After their report, he was able to obtain the cash balance. He even observed that a major chunk was maintained in the current account, in which no interest was paid by the bank. To solve this issue, he opened a flexi account in the bank, in which, after a certain level, night balance is kept as a fixed deposit in the bank, which can be used again in the morning. So, by having a close look at the business cycle, Gyanchandra was not only able to get cash flows but also earned money on the fixed deposits done with the banks.

Calculative Risk is Better Than Only Risk

It is always better to have calculative risk because it may help you to know the maximum losses you may incur. Researcher Sally describes "calculated risk taking" in the following way:

"Calculated risk-taking is operationally defined as the ability to deal with incomplete information and act on a risky option, that requires skill, to actualise challenging but realistic goals."

Some of the ways to calculate risk can be:

- Research – Evaluate commercial potentiality from every perspective
- Anticipate Mistakes - Think about every possible outcome, both positive as well as negative
- Set Milestones and Goals
- Measure Continuity, etc.

Benefits of taking calculative risk are noteworthy. It helps you in taking better decisions, providing time for balancing self, understanding and preparing for maximum loss scheme. All this is possible only by planning well. If not done properly, then it may generate a situation of crisis.

Another stakeholder cited the following case study for better understanding:

Ashish was having a multi-chain restaurant. As he had to face immense struggle to reach this level, he wanted to have a safe and optimised business. However, he always cared for the crisis management and frequently asked himself what if it failed. Just when his business picked up pace and he was about to clear his dues, unexpectedly, COVID-19 hit the country. Every profitable business started turning into losses. Ashish was also on the list; his optimisation and crisis management had failed, or so he thought. He was being pressurised by the landlords for paying the rents even though his revenue was nil. Though he was not having any fruitful idea to save himself from the situation, before paying rent, he reviewed all rent agreements. To his relief, he found the clause that in case of government lockdowns, no rent would have to be paid. This proved to be a huge respite, and he was able to save the rent till the official government lockdown continued. Thus, his constant belief in considering crisis management made it possible for him to sustain his business in spite of the miserable circumstances.

Prepare for Crisis

The reason to prepare for crisis is to maintain business continuity and face COVID-19 like situation, due to which, business had to face severe crisis and many businesses failed. Provision should be made such that the day-to-day crisis can be avoided. For this, an entrepreneur should have some spare funds, important machinery belts or spare parts, and other resources, the absence of which can hamper the working of the company. Not only pandemics, there can be other emergency situations as well which can stall your work; like the supplier may be having some crisis and unable to deliver on time, or an important personnel may be on leave, or any other unexpected situation. Crisis can only be managed by maintaining and reviewing reserves on a regular basis. If it is not done efficiently with change in business situations, then business continuity may hamper.

Enlarged Family, Living Life for Others

After you set up a business, you shoulder the responsibility of an enlarged family, owing to the number of stakeholders. You feel satisfied and motivated from within to do exceptional work for yourself, stakeholders, and even the government. You become a pillar for the government, which helps in the development of the country as well.

Let us overview who all are a part of the business family now:

- Family
- Promoters
- Investors
- Stakeholders
- Government entity
- Bank
- Consultants
- Employees

You should always keep in mind how the business is paying back to such an enlarged family and how many people are dependent on this business set-up. You need to realise that now you have to maintain it not only for yourself but also for the enlarged family.

Summary:

- Business network is an important network which works for you. You need to understand how you can get maximum benefits out of it.
- In any case, keep your trade secrets to yourself, because it is the X factor of your business. Share it wisely so that the competitor does not create obstacles in your growth.
- Always keep reserves for crisis, because business is consistently at risk due to innumerable circumstances, which are mostly out of your control. To safeguard your business against the risk, creating reserves like funds and important resources, is crucial.

Activities:

- Prepare a set of ethics that you will never compromise while in business.
- List down your networks and discuss your plans with them to have a better version of your idea.
- Calculate the risk of plans that you are going to execute.
- Thank your enlarged family who will or who has contributed to your success.

Conclusion

A man of dreams as big as the sky, with immense potential and inert ability to soar high – This is how Sachin would define Paras when he would look at him with pride for all that he had achieved so far. The Paras, who was unconfident, lacking in skills, clueless about how to conduct a business, had come a long way from being a house-help to the director of a large manufacturing unit. Not only did he prove to the ex-employer who had insulted him, but he also managed to achieve success that many could only dream of. Once he started on the journey, he didn't give up, learning along the way, upgrading his abilities, gaining knowledge, expanding his network, learning the ropes of business at every step of the way. Today, Paras has achieved beyond his expectations, yet, not even for a minute has he forgotten his roots. His endeavour is to reach out to people, elevate their lifestyle, and impart to them knowledge and skills, is appreciable.

Also, he is indebted to Sachin, who was the first person to believe in his capabilities. Without him, he wouldn't have achieved his aspirations. And for this reason, he is taking care of Sachin even today. Sachin eventually relocated out of India, in a pollution-free environment so that his kidney would function without any issues. Paras continues to lend him monetary help and whatever other help is required by Sachin. On the other hand, the consultant and the banker continued to be his guiding angels. The consultant is now well known for his startup ideas, while the banker has been promoted to be the General Manager of the bank, owing to his understanding of the basic needs of the MSME business. They were now a team, supporting each other. Paras' motive finally got fulfilled and the urge to serve the society with high quality and healthy variant of rice. This made his life a grand success.

Till date, Paras' success journey continues, as he has established multiple manufacturing units. His exemplary life has motivated many to be undeterred by the challenges life would throw at you and keep achieving one milestone after another, and spread your wings to reach unprecedented heights.

• • •

You can reach author at hrkpankaj@gmail.com

* 9 7 9 8 8 8 9 7 5 2 7 9 0 *